MY RUSSIAN YESTERDAYS

CATHERINE DE HUECK

My Russian Yesterdays

THE BRUCE PUBLISHING COMPANY
MILWAUKEE

COPYRIGHT, 1951, CATHERINE DE HUECK
MADE IN THE UNITED STATES OF AMERICA

Dedicated to

GEORGE . . . PENNY . . . KATIA . . . and PETER

FOREWORD

Do not, dear friends, expect this book to be controversial or startling in its political, economic, or historical revelations. It is none of these things. It is just a simple book that attempts no more than merely to live up to its title. It is simply a series of sketches or vignettes of the everyday life of the ordinary Russian people, and of the role their faith played in that life.

The word *faith* is perhaps the key to the whole book. For I want to show the deep, abiding faith of my people in God and the things of God as it was "then" and as I firmly believe it is even "now" in the deep underground of their hearts and souls.

Also I believe that the example of this simple yet profound faith may help us in this modern, complex, and fearsome world to find our way back to the peace and tranquillity of God's order!

The customs, celebrations, prayers, and the "ways of doing things" that you will find in these pages were common to both Catholic and Orthodox in Russia. In those days, Poland, Lithuania, and a great part of Catholic Ukraine officially formed part and parcel of "Russia." Unofficially, intermarriage, the close living together of neighbors, the influx of Russians into the Catholic parts of the country and vice versa — all had their effects. Then, too, one must remember that the Reformation and its fruits hardly touched the vast Russian lands.

Catholic and Orthodox believers were alike in nearly everything. There was almost no Protestantism in the land. Easily, therefore, you will find many pre-Reformation customs prevailing in Russia that once were common to all Christendom. In the West somehow they got lost "in the shuffle." I give them to you as they came to me, from living with my grandmother's folks near Warsaw; and with my grandfather's near Moscow.

To Our Lady of Fatima I offer these simple pages . . . for she knows how much and how deeply she was (and is) loved in Russia under her hundred titles. This is why she is asking prayers for the land that made *The Bogoroditza* the woof and warp of its whole life.

For should Russia come all the way home to her Father's Inner Room, who knows but that she may lead the rest of the world back to Christ? She will have learned many things on the way to Gethsemani . . . in the taste of the bitter cup . . . and in the outlines of the world, as seen from the Cross.

Hasn't she already sipped from the bitter chalice of persecution . . . drunk it to its bloody dregs? Hasn't she hung on a cross of Communist-making for more than three decades?

And are not suffering and death, meekly borne, the way to the Resurrection?

Our Lady of Fatima, save the land of my people. Bring them back to you. All the way back. Let Russia be openly *yours* again. Let her once more be covered with your shrines, whose slender tapers, set before your ikons, will be the light of the world. Amen.

CONTENTS

Foreword		vii
CHAPTER		
One	Bogoroditza	1
Two	At Home	7
Three	We Bake Bread	15
Four	We Clean House	20
Five	The Herbs We Used	25
Six	The Work of Our Hands	31
Seven	The Fulness Thereof	39
Eight	On Pilgrimage	47
Nine	Christmas in Old Russia	54
Ten	Easter in Old Russia	60
Eleven	We Pray	66
Twelve	I Take Thee	74
Thirteen	May the Soul	84
Fourteen	Village Life	90
Fifteen	Co-operatives	104
Sixteen	Education	107
Seventeen	Sports	117
Eighteen	Recreation	121
Nineteen	Customs	125

MY RUSSIAN YESTERDAYS

Chapter One

BOGORODITZA

The devotion to the Bogoroditza, which, in Russian, means "She who gave birth to God," came to its vastness, it is said, in the heart of a beautiful Russian princess, St. Olga, who, in the ninth century, journeyed far across the sea to the golden city of Constantinople-by-the-Bosphorus to be baptized.

Be that as it may. One thing is certain. When the Bogoroditza came, with her Son, His Father, and her Spouse, she came to stay, and to rule the Russian hearts unto the end of time. Many are the countries that have been officially dedicated to her; but only in Russia have all the people made her their very own mother, dedicating themselves to her.

The Russian's love for her grew with the growth of the nation. Its history can be read in the litany of titles given her. For wherever the Russians went she seemed to go ahead of them, appearing miraculously, now in this plain, now in that city or stronghold, showering them with blessings. . . . And each time some solitary artist in some hidden monastery would record these happenings with an ikon of her.

Thus . . . the Holy Virgin of Kazan . . . the Blessed Mother of Czestochowa . . . the Bogoroditza of Kiev . . . Tver . . . Novgorod. Behind each ikon is a story that would rival the miracles of Our Lady of Fatima, or of Lourdes.

Like a gossamer fabric, shining, light, but infinitely strong, *She who gave birth to God* covered every nook, every corner, of the Russian land. She covered the people and their lives. Some day historians and artists will discover this, and reveal to the world the rosary of Russian shrines dedicated just to her, because in that immense land there is no city so big, no hamlet so small, as not to have some landmark, some shrine, or some ikon erected to her, the beloved of the people.

It was the Bogoroditza who got every part of Russia acquainted with all the other parts in the old days. Russians, like the rest of her children the world over, turn to her for most of the favors they want from her Son. In return for the immense values they receive from her, and in recognition of their sinfulness and unworthiness, and with warm, deep gratitude, or in further petition to her, they go on a pilgrimage to one of her many shrines.

They go fasting, barefooted, simply clad, chanting her litanies and praising her name. They are well aware of the power of the fasting and the penance they offer through her to the Most Holy Trinity, power given by God Himself, to enable men to untie the hands of His mercy and to appease the hands of His justice. One of the many litanies chanted to her is as follows:

> Hail Mary, mother of God, virgin and mother, morning star, perfect vessel.
> Hail Mary, mother of God, holy temple in which God Himself was conceived.
> Hail Mary, mother of God, chaste and pure dove.
> Hail Mary, mother of God, ever effulgent light; from whom proceedeth the Sun of Justice.
> Hail Mary, mother of God, who didst enclose in thy sacred womb the One who cannot be encompassed.
> Hail Mary, mother of God. With the shepherds we sing the praises of God; and with the angels, the song of thanksgiving: Glory to God in the highest and peace on earth to men of good will.
> Hail Mary, mother of God, through thee came to us the Conqueror, the triumphant Vanquisher of hell.
> Hail Mary, mother of God, through thee blossoms the splendor of the Resurrection.
> Hail Mary, mother of God; thou hast saved every faithful Christian.
> Hail Mary, mother of God; who can praise thee worthily, O blessed, O glorious Virgin Mary?

To each of these invocations the answer is: "We salute thee, mother of God!"

Through these endless, constant pilgrimages, men, women, and children of all social stratas and conditions came together, praising her name, learning to love her and her Son, learning to love one another.

Long ago and far away in the dimness of centuries

gone by, she was given the title, *Mother of the Body of Christ*. This was but another way of expressing the sublime doctrine of the Mystical Body of Christ, which the West lost soon after the Reformation. But Russia, which the Reformation passed by, never lost it. How could she? Her heavenly Mother would not let simple, devout children stray away from the very essence of their faith.

You see the many facets of this faith reflected in Russian literature — through Dostoevski, Tolstoy, Chekhov, and, if the truth be told, even through the present-day writers.

The hunger for justice is the most characteristic trait of the Russian. In his eternal quest for the integration of the doctrine of the Mystical Body of Christ, he may wander even into the heresy of Communism. But, mark well, he will not stay there long, as God reckons time. How could he — who even now loves his Mother so well?

In every Russian home there are many ikons. But the Virgin's ikon always hangs in the eastern corner of the bedroom. And a gently flickering light burns before it, night and day, through the years. It is here that the life of the family begins and ends.

It is to the Bogoroditza that the bridegroom brings his bride. Together they kneel before her gentle face. They ask her benediction on their marital love. They beg her to make it fruitful in the Lord, her Son.

It is to her they pray again, when their love is consummated in the flesh. With the candid manner of childlike trust, they thank her for the infinite blessings of giving — maybe — life to a new soul, which then and there they dedicate to her and her divine Son.

It is before this ikon that the mother prays during

childbirth. It is here that, soon after birth, the child will be brought for a blessing. It is here the child will kneel and pray, when he is old enough, all his little prayers.

Family councils will be held before this ikon. And even death will pay it honor, for it will hear the last whisper of father, mother, or child. The Bogoroditza is the center of the life of this household ... of every household of the land. That's why her ikon hangs in so intimate a place.

The Rosary is known in Russia. But it is considered an extremely holy and high form of prayer to her. Only nuns and monks and a few saintly lay people are allowed to say it, the latter only with the permission of their spiritual directors.

An old and revered custom was to remember Mary in one's will. Czars and commoners, princes and paupers, have willed their best to her in money or precious stones, in silver or gold. That is why most of the well-known ikons in Russian churches were so richly decorated. Each stone, each silver bit, represented either thanks for favors received, or petition for favors.

Those who could not give gold or silver or jewels brought her the works of their hands. Her shrines, in small chapels, on special altars in the bigger churches or in monasteries or convents, were usually decorated with exquisitely embroidered silks and linens that had taken years to make. Fruits and plants were also sometimes seen at her shrine, gifts from grateful farmers.

The old Russian greeting starts with: "May the peace of God be with you," but the farewell is Mary's: "May the blue mantle of our Lady cover you with its gracious folds, and keep you safe."

She permeates the Liturgy. She fills its many ectenes.

She walks through the Mass. She is invoked at the *Panihida*, the prayer for the dead. She is always present in the *Moleben*, the prayer of petition.

Numberless are the songs about her, liturgical and national. It is her ikon that blesses the child. Parental blessings for all occasions are a must in Russian life. Father or mother blesses the child with the ikon, for school, for sickness, for marriage, in the beginning of a search for a job, in any endeavor, in any crisis.

The *Ave* is the prayer the Russians love best. It contains only the angel's greeting. The second part, the "Holy Mary, mother of God . . ." is omitted . . . *Bogoroditza, deva Raduisa. Blagodatnaia Maria, gospod s toboyou. Blagoslovena ti vi jenah blagosloven plod chreva tvoego. . . . Amin.*

Yes, *She who gave birth to God . . . loves Russia . . . and is beloved by Russia. It is to her that all must pray. May she cover the Russians with the blue mantle of her love and bring them safely, in its gracious folds, back to the house of their fathers. . . .*

I, a Russian, pray to her daily for that end. I pray to her under her best known title, *Spouse of the Holy Ghost and Mother of the Father's Word. . . .*

Will you, friends of America, join me in that prayer?

Chapter Two

AT HOME

"*God's peace be upon you . . . and may it abide in you too.*"
How familiar to me, and how beloved, is the memory of this greeting, heard so many times in my childhood and youth!

It must be the constant talks about a vanishing peace that swirl and eddy all about me via radio, newspapers, and magazines that have started me on the road to my Russian yesterdays, a road I have been taking often lately.

Just last night, for instance, my present surroundings

vanished and I was back in our immense apartment in St. Petersburg. It was evening. Dinner was over, the table cleaned. A fire burned cheerily in the big fireplace of our dining room, the favorite room in the house. My brother and I had finished our homework. He was busy drawing some very special pictures of his own. I was sitting on the floor, sewing. Mother was embroidering, and Father was reading the Gospel for the next day's Mass, pausing now and then to explain some obscure passage.

All around the table were the servants, each engaged in some work such as whittling, carving, sewing, embroidering, knitting. Yet all their attention was on what Father was reading and expounding. Now and then someone would ask a question, or nod wisely and understandingly. There was oneness in the group. The oneness of love and belonging.

Suddenly the soft chimes of the front doorbell interrupted the proceedings. The footman rose to answer it. In a few minutes a friend walked in. Turning his face first to the ikon, a holy picture of our blessed Lord, he bowed low three times, thus greeting the unseen but ever present Master of the house. Then turning to all of us, and bowing again, he said, "God's peace be upon you all."

In unison we answered, "And may it abide in you too."

This Christian greeting was so commonplace in my childhood that it is no wonder that all this talk about vanishing peace brought it back to me. Only, strangely, in my childhood there *was* peace — a deep, inner peace that no one could take away from us. I feel sure that this "peace" is still in the hearts of all Russia's children today — greater, maybe, than even in my days, because it has been paid for with the precious coin of sufferings.

At Home

But all around me, here, today, there is no peace. Perhaps this is because we have forgotten its Source . . . perhaps because we do not greet one another any more in His name, nor wish one another His peace. . . .

Home? Home was several places to me. One was this big apartment in town where we spent our winters. There were fourteen servants to keep it clean, to attend to the great deal of entertainment that went with my father's job, and to minister to our wants, which was the smallest part of their work.

Notwithstanding this big labor force, I was not allowed, by any manner of means, to live the life of the "idle rich." On the contrary, I had to help the servants to serve and, in the process, to learn every household task they performed.

It was not that my parents thought their daughter should be a household drudge or confine herself to the kitchen. Far from it. Their concept of Christian life included that of the dignity of work. All kinds of work. And all workers. It also embraced all vocations open to a woman.

According to their concept, marriage, the religious life, or spinsterhood — at home or in a career — each would benefit and be enhanced by a factual knowledge of household tasks and other manual labors suited to the strength and ability of a woman.

I think that always before their eyes was the life of Mary, "She who gave birth to God," the Queen of Heaven, who cooked and wove and washed and scrubbed, yet was learned in Holy Scriptures and wise with the wisdom of both God and man.

Yes, even as other parents in Russia, they wanted to give their daughter the heritage of knowledge; many types of knowledge. First was the knowledge of God; then, according to one's state in life, academic schooling and the like, the arts, which included music, and handicrafts, especially needlecraft. Then the art of making and managing a home, prudently, efficiently, graciously, and in the spirit of Christ and His beloved Mother.

So my life was a full one with going to school, and learning a thousand things outside of its scope; not out of books, but by doing them over and over again. The procedure was a simple one. First, I had to take care of my own room and things. Then I "filled-in" on the day off of every female domestic except the cook! And slowly I was being made ready even for that.

Thus it was that I learned, at firsthand, how to launder fine table linens, starch them just so, and iron them slowly until nary a wrinkle showed; and how to fold them then, meticulously and uniformly, as well as beautifully. I learned, too, how to set a table with them, and with the sparkling silver and glassware, washed and polished until it caught every light; for the family first, then for guests, maybe a party of ten; then, later, a party of twenty-five; finally graduating to the supertype, held once or twice in the house, of fifty or more.

In the sweat of my brow, and through a thousand aches and pains, I finally found out how to keep kitchen utensils clean, knives sharp, and floors and tables scrubbed until their white pine wood rivaled snow.

A day came when I truly enjoyed the sight of clean and evenly cut vegetables, all ready, in their cold-water bath, for the stove and dinner to come, adding color and sunshine to the drab gray mornings while they waited to be cooked. It even became a game for me to prepare vegetables for the big dinners, when many of them had to be cut in fancy shapes, and carrots and turnips became roses and a variety of other flowers under my now expert ministrations. So did the butter. I delighted in molding it into a thousand fancy shapes.

Painfully came the lessons of mending and darning. It seems as if the holes in the stockings and socks were alive with perversity. They just would not become the neatly mended, almost invisibly rewoven squares my mother demanded.

Patches on linen towels, sheets, napkins, and tablecloths were sheer penances to me. But eventually I mastered this art of keeping things repaired. It even came to pass that I began to like the eternal struggle between me and the disruptive ways of time.

Waiting on table was always fun. But to be sure of which side one waited from — what cutlery went with what — which spoon went with this or that — took a long time. But I developed observance and speed.

Minding my baby brother, on nurse's day off was another joy and this was like entering a universe of diapers, baths, baby foods, and milk bottles that had to be warmed up just right.

Yes, taking the place of waitress, kitchen or scullery maid, baby's nurse, governess, seamstress, and laundress, on their days off, was an education which I would not have missed for the world. It taught me every branch of house management, by doing them.

It served me well, this training, when, penniless, I came to this new world. But it did more. It gave me a living, a start. It built self-assurance in me and confidence. I needed both desperately. It also brought me the deep and profound understanding of the dignity of *all work and all workers.*

It made me see, long before I ever heard of the existence of Eric Gill, that indeed, in a Christian home, in a Christian family, in a Christian State, *all things go together.*

Home? Home was also our big estate — the farm on which we spent the springs and summers and early falls. I loved its old sprawling house, its herb room and workroom, its milk cellars and pantries, its old barns, and its orchards and fields.

In these surroundings, other duties came to me. Mother was a splendid practical nurse. Twice a week she went into the villages to nurse the sick and the poor. I was her assistant. I would like to have a penny for every mile I walked, carrying a heavy knapsack containing medicines and first-aid needs, for the floors, windows, and doors I scrubbed, for the beds I made in sickrooms.

Early in my childhood, the truth that Christ is in my neighbor was shown to me by my parents' example and words.

No one was ever turned from our door, bum or beggar, woman of the streets or thief. The men were welcomed by my father. He gave them a bath, himself, or Mother would do it for the women; then they would be given clothing if they needed it. They would be served by Mother and Father and by us children — *if we had been good through the week*, and thus worthy of serving Christ in the poor — on our best linen and from our best china in the main dining room.

It is thus that we children learned the precious lesson of LOVING OUR NEIGHBOR AS OURSELVES AND TO PROVE, THROUGH SERVING THEM, OUR LOVE TO GOD.

But studying, working, helping and serving the poor was not all our life. There was so much gaiety, so much joy in our lives, that somehow it brings tears to my eyes when I behold my own inability to transmit even a little bit of it to the youth of today. How I wish I could! For it would bring so much happiness, so much *peace* into their lives, into the lives of their parents, into their communities, and — who can tell? — into the whole world!

Our joys, our gladness, our fun came from within. They sprang from that sense of security, love, and belonging, which our parents gave us so lavishly. They came, too, from the sense of Order. I spell it deliberately with a capital "O" because it stems from the great and tranquil ORDER OF GOD HIMSELF.

When the life of an individual or a family is rooted in that great tranquillity of God's order, when its ends are Christocentric, and Faith is an essential part of it, then joy, true laughter, and real gaiety flower abundantly in that individual's or that family's life. Then children grow up in an atmosphere of love and tenderness. Where love is, God is.

And so our fun was simple. Oh, the anguishing moments we experienced in writing plays and producing them; we and our neighbors' children. And the pride of achievement when our parents and friends really liked both script and production.

Have you ever really treasure-hunted in the long twilight evenings of the North? That game is worth a thousand modern "Monopolies" or "Canastas." Clues are planted all over, and the treasure hunt takes you into beauty spots hard to match, or to forget. Of course, it also gives you a chance to meet, for a second or two, the one who makes your heart beat faster. But alas, there are so many around that you won't be alone for long!

Or have you danced under the stars on the threshing

floor of a big, open barn to the tune of old violins? . . . Or played charades? . . . No? . . . I'm sorry you missed all that.

Our home was not only a place of work, it also was the natural abode of peace and laughter and love.

And who can say that all this did not come from the constant greeting that was exchanged by so many, so often in our home — *"God's peace be upon you . . . and may it abide in you too."*

> Mother of Christ,
> Keeper of St. Joseph's house,
> Heart of all hearths,
> Patroness of all wives and mothers,
> Give me the grace
> To make a home
> Wherever I am.
> Amen.

Chapter Three

WE BAKE BREAD

It was Friday, and Friday was always a very special day in our house and in those of our neighbors, for it was "bread-setting day." The big kitchen was immaculate. The bread table, the worktable were scrubbed to a dazzling white; and the big table at which the help ate was covered with a tablecloth, finely embroidered in cross-stitch and of many vivid hues.

The big wood-burning range was warm, and the cat and her kittens were curled up as close to it as they could get. The vigil light before the big ikon flickered, and its flicker was reflected in, it seemed to me, a hundred shining copper pans which hung in orderly rows on the whitewashed walls and made pools of light, often too bright to look at long.

The shelves that ran all along the walls were filled with beautifully wrought jars and jugs. Local craftsmen made them out of special clay, decorated them with original designs, and baked them in old-fashioned kilns. These kept the strangely blended vegetable dyes for centuries.

I loved the jars both for their beauty and their contents which always amazed me. They seemed to contain an inexhaustible supply of wonderful things — sweet-smelling herbs, strange roots and barks, cookies, spiced sugars and plums, an infinite variety of dried vegetables — in short, a world of secrets to delight any child's heart.

But I was not allowed much time to spend with these jars for my help was needed. The cook and Mother were bringing out the big, heavy, wooden bread tubs. These were washed but twice a year. Ordinarily they were just wiped with a clean piece of cloth and tightly covered with another until needed again. In each there was always left a lumpy piece of dough the size of a fist. This seemed to me to be a part of the tub. But it was really only the "leaven."

The flour bins were opened. Rye flour that smelled so good! Whole-wheat flour, ground rough in the local mills, that made such a nourishing wholesome bread! White flour for Sunday and holyday breads! There they all were in big bins, blending with each other. The staff of life that made men work from dawn to dusk. How beautiful they were!

The water was warmed just so, and now was the time to pray. On our knees, on the scrubbed pine floor, we prayed first to the Lord Christ:

We Bake Bread

"O Lord Jesus Christ, Bread of angels, Living Bread unto eternal life, bless this bread, as Thou didst bless the five loaves in the wilderness: that all who eat it with reverence may through it attain the corporal and spiritual health they desire. Who livest and reignest eternally. Amen."

Then to His Blessed Mother, for wasn't she the Patroness of the Home, and wasn't breadmaking the sacramental of the home? So naturally it had to be talked over with her. Her Son's blessing on the ready bread was essential, but hers was needed too, to get flour and water, salt and sugar together so that there would be a palatable loaf!

Now the tubs themselves were blessed with the sign of the cross, and then the bakers blessed themselves. All was ready to set the dough.

Slowly, reverently, flour and water were mixed into a thin batter. The tubs were put on the tile edge of the range, then covered; first with a clean linen cloth, then with old clean blankets.

Another sign of the cross would be made for good rising . . . and the women would leave the kitchen on tiptoes.

The cat and I would stay, both curled up near the warm stove, in the dimness of the cozy shining kitchen. As often as not we would both fall asleep there, the cat for the second time, and I for the first. Two hours later, Mother and cook would be back to add the rest of the flour and whatever spice, sugar, butter, or eggs had to go into the special dough.

Slowly, with a long wooden paddle, they again mixed the whole. Then they began kneading it, their elbows going deep into the dough until the dough would fall off their hands and arms. Then the batch was ready for "sleep."

Rye bread takes a long time to "rise." Tomorrow morning it would be ready for the next operation.

And tomorrow could never come soon enough for me. Week after week, fascinated, I watched. Somehow, that baking was "home" to me. Always, when bread was made, I felt at home. It was like a ritual, all tied up with God and His cross, and the Blessed Mother.

Now it was tomorrow. When I came downstairs, the baking oven — which in all Russian kitchens formed the back part of every stove — was filled with glowing coals, which soon would be raked out into the stove. The things I saw in those glowing coals! They would fill many a fairy book. Coals have that way with me. They stir my imagination.

Mother and cook were already hard at work on the dough. They had kneaded it again, thrown it about the long pine table, put it once more to rise, but this time on big sheets of tin. Russians seldom use tins to bake their bread in; they just put big lumps on the sheet and let them spread in round appetizing loaves. They rise a while on these, and then are gently picked up on a flat wooden shovel and thrust, in orderly rows, into the baking oven.

And what a heavenly smell issued from that oven! I can still smell it . . . and feel all the ecstasy of my childhood.

Hours later, round brown loaves would be placed on the back of the baking oven on a white sheet and covered with blankets for the day.

Saturday evening would bring a supper of milk, cottage cheese, and freshly baked bread with homemade butter. What restaurant could beat that?

And let me tell you about the part bread plays at a wedding! In Russia, the couple just married are met by the father of the bride, carrying a loaf of bread on a wooden platter, and by the mother, carrying salt. These are symbols of the material and spiritual welfare that is wished for them. The bread typifies material goods, the salt spiritual goods. "For you are the salt of the earth."

Bread plays such a great role in the lives of the Russians! It is to them, indeed, the holy staff of life.

Soldiers' rations, for instance, include two and a half pounds of bread per meal. It is *the* meal.

Even now, thousands of miles away from Russia, I often startle friends walking with me — and I certainly puzzle passers-by — because, when I see a piece of bread lying on the street or sidewalk, I pick it up, kiss it, bless myself, and put it on some ledge near by, away from dirty shoes.

This is an old Russian custom.

The Russians revere bread because the Son of Man chose it as His Substance for us.

Chapter Four

WE CLEAN HOUSE

The Sunday paper is full of ads about materials and short cuts for spring cleaning. Through the open window I can hear, above the noises of the traffic, two birds quarreling. The nasturtiums I planted two weeks ago in the window boxes are coming up. Definitely spring is here.

The paper lies at my feet, unheeded. The sounds of traffic and the quarreling of the birds barely reach my consciousness. Again I have journeyed into my yesterdays, this time, into that special, that *very* special, week when we cleaned house.

We Clean House

There were few short cuts to the work in those days, and if there had been any, I don't think they would have been accepted. For we looked on work as a hallowed occupation, blessed by the ways of centuries past, to be started in God, for God, and with a prayer to God. The home was the symbol of Christ and His Church, and the cleaning thereof was something holy; to be done according to customs, which, perhaps unconsciously, took the place of rubrics.

Also it was fun. We made most of our cleaning materials ourselves. And the preparations for that important week started almost a year ahead. First there had to be a survey, of course; for, in all things of life, the Russian housewife believed there must be order, the tranquillity of order.

So, with paper and pencil, each room would be gone over, and the work to be done noted down and divided into the days at hand. Laundering, dyeing, scrubbing, washing, polishing, airing — each had its turn, its proper place. And the making ready for each was a task apart.

For instance, there was the question of curtains. Everyone knows that these fade through the year. So they had to be redyed. And that would bring us to the summer, to the gathering of flowers and roots from which we would make the vegetable dyes for the faded curtains next spring. What fun it used to be!

Up with sunrise. A hot, full breakfast. Everyone gathering with baskets and linen bags, ready for the day. Mother reciting a prayer to St. Martha, the patron saint of the home. Off we would go, several miles down the road, into the fields and forests that held the precious plants we needed for the day's work.

I always chose the fields and the collecting of cornflowers. I loved to walk through the golden wheat fields where they made their home. There they were. Vividly blue. Beckoning to me. Here, there, and everywhere. It was a pity they had to be squeezed into a linen bag that hung over my shoulder. But still it was fun to gather them.

They give such a lovely shade of blue too, to the materials dyed. I have never found that exact shade since. Somehow, it always made me think of our Lady's gown. I wager it was just that beautiful soft shade of cornflower blue. . . .

To get this blue we used to put the cornflowers into gallon bottles filled with alcohol and let them stand until almost the next spring, on the sunniest window of the house.

Other flowers and roots we mashed and boiled, filtering their coloring into dark brown, slender bottles for next spring's needs. The New York Public Library has a little book on vegetable dyes that, positively, has the ability to make me homesick.

Then there was the brass and copper to clean. All the kitchen utensils were made of those metals in my young days. That meant polishing and then some! But what a beautiful, gorgeous sight is a spotless kitchen with shelf upon shelf of gleaming brass and copper!

Frankly, I never saw "BRASSO" or other similar cleaning aids until I came to America, yet I have cleaned positively thousands of pots and pans. For this we used bread. Ordinary rye bread. Gathering the leftovers, the crusts, we soaked them in a little water, allowing them to become sour and ferment. With this "mush" we cleaned the copper and the brass. And *does* it clean? It surely *does!*

We Clean House

For all the endless washing and scrubbing that Russian housewives love so, one needs pounds and pounds of soap. We made our own, naturally. So there was the collecting of fats and the boiling of them with lye. And again, to me, every step in the art of making soap was fun.

St. Martha was there, of course. You brought her there with a little prayer. If you forgot, that was just too bad. The soap would be too dry, or too soft, as sure as you were alive. Only those who have made soap know the joy of cutting it into tidy, soft, large squares, and putting the cakes into the sun to dry.

Floors were polished with wax. Hard floors, that is. We had our own beehives, and so our own wax, for floors, for candles, and for vigil lights. Mother used to make the candles. The special prayers that go with each were beautiful but hard to translate.

Waxmaking started, as all works did, with the sign of the cross. *In the name of the Father, and of the Son, and of the Holy Ghost....*

The soft white pine floors were scrubbed, not with a floor brush but with brooms made out of birch branches that had been gathered the year before and dried in the barn. Some leaves would still be clinging to them and smelling sweet and "green" when immersed in hot water. They made a grand "brush" to scrub floors with. And they went well with the homemade soap and the clean yellow sand. The floors came out dazzling white....

Mending and sewing was, of course, an important part of spring cleaning. I loved the sewing room, with its big ikon of our Blessed Mother of Kazan, before which burned an extra big vigil light, its two sewing machines, its long cutting tables. From the ceiling rafters hung, in orderly rows, linen threads made of our own flax and dyed with our own dyes, and long skeins of wool from our own sheep, also dyed at home.

Yes, the preparation for spring cleaning began a year ahead. And after it was all over, each room would be sprinkled with holy water. Then we would all go to the steam bath, wash thoroughly, and go to confession and Communion, returning to a breakfast of tea with thick cream, freshly made buns, and raspberry jam!

That paper lying at my feet. . . . How varied are the short cuts and the cleansing materials it offers! How varied and how dull! Because of them, much of the fun and the joy and the satisfaction of cleaning a house have gone, never, perhaps, to return.

Chapter Five

THE HERBS WE USED

THERE is one place in the modern department store that has a special fascination for me. That is the "herb" department, usually a rather tiny and overdecorated part of the grocery section.

Always I have to visit it, though I know it will bring a flood of memories and make me so homesick for the happy days of my childhood that I will have to leave it on the run, handicapped with tear-filled eyes. Yet, I always end up in that spicy corner of the sales emporium.

But I am usually a rather lonely visitor, wandering among the beautiful jars, the sachets, the gay containers of culinary herbs. For it seems that the love, knowledge, and lore of herbs belongs to a forgotten page of history.

True, it is being slowly resurrected. Here and there one sees articles about herbs, for seasoning, for keeping linens sweet, for adding fragrance to dainty clothing. But there is so little life to it all! It is much simpler and much cheaper to go to a drugstore and buy this chemical scent or that elusive perfume — made from coal tar — than to seek the genuine article.

But how much joy is lost by this indifference!

When one lives about eighty miles from a railroad, as we did once upon a time, and there are no Sears-Roebuck or Montgomery-Ward or T. Eaton catalogues to be had, and doctors and nurses are far away in time of epidemic — then herbs become very important in the life of a man, or a community. And those who knew herbs and could use them to cure sickness, to keep meats longer, to make meals tastier, or to add fragrance to life in general, were much respected and loved by their neighbors. Their fame traveled far and wide.

My mother was one of those people. From early childhood she loved the sick. Perhaps it came to her naturally, for her father and grandfather were physicians. She used to tell me that she pored over the books of *Materia Medica* that filled their shelves. They were old books and full of information about herbs.

She remembered the big medicine room of her grandfather, where he often made up his own medicines from herbs bought from "Herb Men," people who spent their lives in the wilds gathering medicinal herbs for doctors. In those days many M.D.'s brewed their own medicines.

Her father, more advanced in medical ways than his forebears, retained a healthy respect for these old and tried folkway medicines and used them quite often.

But perhaps Mother learned still more from the peasants among whom she spent her youth. Old men and women were her favorites. She could sit by the hour, listening to their medical lore, and gathering and writing down their recipes. She learned more than medicine from them. She learned the secrets of spicing bread, soups, meats, and salads, of adding a tang and a zest to drinks, and of giving a fresh beauty and fragrance to clothes.

Little by little she learned to nurse the sick. Little by little her fame grew, and it was her turn to pass on to others the knowledge that had been given her.

As soon as I was able to undertake the fairly long journeys she regularly made to the various villages in our neighborhood, I was drafted. I was "Mother's little helper."

She would give me a knapsack full of medicines and bandages to carry, and would sometimes allow me to aid with the nursing. But mostly my job consisted in helping to clean the houses of the sick; prepare light, nourishing meals; take care of the children for a while; make beds; and the like.

I liked that. But the real red-letter days of my life were herb-gathering days. These were "special." They embraced all the seasons except winter. I could write a book on the beauty and joy of the long walks those days entailed.

Three times a week we went a-gathering. Like everything else in old Russia, the occasion had to be started with prayer. So, before setting out, in the early morning, in that strange hour before the dew had completely dried — herbs had to be gathered rightly according to moon cycles and times of day — Mother and I, and such others as made up the party, would kneel and recite the prayer that has stayed with me all through these years:

> Almighty, everlasting God, by Thy word alone Thou hast made heaven and earth, and all things visible and invisible, and hast adorned the earth with plants and trees for the use of men and animals. Thou appointest each species to bring forth fruit in its kind, not only to serve as food for living creatures, but also as medicine for sick bodies.
>
> With mind and body we earnestly implore Thine unutterable goodness to bless these various herbs and add to their natural powers the grace of Thy new blessing. May they ward off disease and adversity from men and beasts who use them in Thy name. Through our Lord Jesus Christ, Thy Son, who liveth and reigneth with Thee in the unity of the Holy Spirit, God forever and ever. Amen.
>
> Bogoroditza . . . Mother of God . . . walk with us . . . bless our search . . . bless us and keep us safe. . . . Amen.

The prayers finished, our lunch safely packed in a linen bag, another bag hanging crosswise from the first, over chest and back, we were off.

Over the winding country road, into the meadows we went; across brooks and ice-blue rushing streamlets, passing in and out of woods, now a whole mile of aromatic pines, now a mile or two of birches that looked like dancing girls dressed in white and green, waiting for the ballet master's sign to leap into a farandole of their own.

There were herbs everywhere. Each species had to be gathered separately and tied in a bunch. Roots had to be put into the linen bags. Leaves were strung together with a big wooden needle and made into necklaces. All were brought to a certain meadow or some other place agreed upon. All our excursions and searches went off from this central "depot" like rays from the sun.

The Herbs We Used

The names of the herbs were to me like a rosary of grace and always my mind came back to the starting prayer. God made this herb to be used to feed or to heal. We were gathering it for that purpose. Surely the blessing would descend upon us too. I would often look up into the blue sky, almost expecting the blessing to come down on me, "like a gentle shower on the fleece." Listen to the rosary of the herbs.

Monkshood. A saintly name for a plant that can be used for powerful medicines. Its roots are best. They can quiet a sick heart — or kill it, if carelessly used.

Churchsteeple. Its leaves make a good astringent for sore throats and also produce the goldenest yellow dies for linens and wool.

Angelica. Its roots make tea that will stop a cough, or poultices for lung and chest diseases. Its stems and stalks, candied, make a lovely dessert. The whole herb can be used to flavor fish.

Our Lady's Bedstraw. Its roots make a bright red dye. Its stem and leaf curdles milk for cheese. Its flower will color butter yellow and will help skin disease and epilepsy.

Holy Thistle. This will cool a fever, become a tonic.

Camomile. Its little flower heads, used in a rinse, will make any blond hair goldener. Made into a tea, it will keep off insects or act as a sedative.

Like a lilting song the names come back to my mind. And I see myself, scanning the edges of brooks, now climbing hazardous rocks, now sitting on green grass, getting my herbs by the handful.

A breeze. The song of a bird. The rustle of leaves. Infinite joy and peace! That was herb-gathering time.

One learned much about plants — but somehow much more about God.

AAAAA ... OUOUOUOU ... the lunch call re-echoed loudly through the woods. Gathering my little harvest together, I ran to the appointed place. Already water boiled merrily in a huge blackened kettle, and Mother was busy with the teapot. Black bread. Fresh butter thickly spread on it. Homemade cheese. And tea. And all around us the unforgettable, almost overpowering, fragrance of gathered herbs.

A short nap, then more walking, peering, bending, gathering, and it was time for going home. On the road a horse and a dray would be waiting for us, and probably a crowd of village kids. We would go home slowly, singing all the folk tunes we knew.

On the morrow, the herbs would be brought into the big workroom, where Mother and I would start sorting them out. Roots here. Leaves there. Stems over there. Be very sure which is which, and from what plant. Check — recheck. Label. Tie these in bunches to hang from rafters. Put the leaves of these to dry in the sun. Keep these leaves and roots fresh, for medicines, dyes, or condiments.

The smells of that room! Will I ever forget them? It seems to me that all nature's fragrance was imprisoned there. There was nothing alien, nothing false. Everything was authentic, pure — everything was straight from the hands of God. There was indeed a blessing on each leaf, on each stem, on each root.

Heaven must be filled with some such fragrance. I was sure of that!

I always maintained, too, that our culinary herb garden, which occupied almost half an acre, smelled better than a flower garden. With marjoram, tarragon, rosemary, thyme, sage, basil, fennel, summer savory, borage, and other delightful aromas, how could it be otherwise?

Chapter Six

THE WORK OF OUR HANDS

THERE was warmth and sunshine in the air. Spring was here, and everyone was talking about the coming of the "wool-men," the shearers of sheep who went from farm to farm, to cut the heavy, woolen, winter coats off the animals before they were led to their distant summer pastures.

To me it was one of the most exciting times of the year. For things began to happen, and fast. The kitchen was a beehive of activity, for the "wool-men" ate even more than the threshers! And so mounds of bread, cheese, and butter had to be made ready.

A cow was slaughtered for the special stew goulash that

always made up the main course of any meal. Salted pork was brought out of its barrels and, rinsed and parboiled, was ready to fill any void that might have been left by the hearty stew. *Pirogies* — yeast dough, well rolled out and filled with meat, onion, stewed cabbage, or mushrooms — were baked and set aside.

Cooks and maids dashed in and out of cellars, barns, pantries, and the kitchen, vivid skirts flying, their heavily embroidered aprons filled to bursting.

And I? I was in the midst of it all.

Daily I would sneak into the big stockade that held the sheep during the winter, and to which they were, at this time of the year, brought back nightly from their near-by pastures. I spent hours admiring the heavy coats of the sheep and wondering why they did not die from exposure without them. I wondered, too, how it was that this matted, dirty wool could become the fleecy, soft, white mass we would soon be spinning.

At long last the "wool-men" came. They heralded their arrival from afar with lusty songs. All was ready for them. The hayloft became their sleeping quarters, the kitchen their dining and living room, the big outdoor pump their bathroom.

On the morning of their arrival, they, and the whole family with them, would go to Mass. This most important part of the farmer's life had to be started with prayer. And what better prayer is there than the Mass?

After Mass, the priest would journey back with us to bless the sheep in their stockade, and the workers outside it; to bless the wool that it might be good to spin, to weave, and to sell; to bless the workers that they might do their work speedily and well and without harm to themselves or the stock.

Prayers over, breakfast finished, the work began in earnest.

Into the big-roofed shed without walls, and onto its heavy, age-old oak floor, the shepherds would bring the sheep, and hold them securely while the wool-men worked on them. In the twinkling of an eye the bleating animals would be coatless and back in the stockade!

This went on all day with the precision of clockwork. In the meantime other men would take the wool in carts to yet another shed. There, big oak troughs were ready and filled with water. The water was constantly changed. Here the wool would be washed over and over again until it was snowy white. Then it would be put on a strange contraption to dry — a sort of huge net made out of narrow strips of hide, attached to poles which stood about four feet apart and about four or five feet from the ground.

The making of this "net" was an art in itself. The hides were cured, dried, and cut into narrow strips during the long winter months. Then they were softened with lard and rubbed with lard to a luster. Early in the spring, they were woven and nailed to their big frames, after which the frames were fastened to the poles.

There the wool would stay, under a high roof built over the net, until it was soft and thoroughly dry.

At night the wool-men would make a big bonfire and sing old Russian songs or tell age-old folk tales. It was there that I learned many songs and stories. There was about these evenings an enchantment that years have not lessened.

Then, as suddenly as they had come, the wool-men were gone. The most glamorous part of spring was gone. Even the echoes of their songs were gone!

The sheep would be taken out of their stockade to their summer pastures; and the dry wool would be put into the carding room.

How few people today know the joy of handling white, clean-smelling wool and of watching it become a beautiful soft piece of cloth! How few people can say that any piece of cloth is the work of their own hands, mind, and imagination! How few of us today know the gladness and the joy of creative achievement that comes with turning raw wool into material for a suit of clothes, a dress, or the habit of a nun?

Carding can be fun, and was, in my Russian yesterdays. For it was a party. Girls and women from the village would come, bringing their own carding combs. The big carding room, with its wide hand-hewn benches standing along the walls, would be filled with laughter and song as busy hands carded the tangled white wool.

Mountains of it, fine, clean, and ready to spin, would soon form on the clean floor. Tall tales were told. The latest village news was exchanged. Everyone talked as she worked.

But as usual, it began with prayer . . . and with prayer it ended.

The carding finished, there would be a dance under the stars, outdoor tables loaded with goodies and nice strong tea. The boys had been patiently waiting for the girls to come out. Now the fiddler would strike up a lively tune, and young feet would dance easily the intricate steps of folk or square dances.

It would be almost dawn when the young people went home, leaving behind them yet another step accomplished in the transformation of the gray, matted wool into a work of beauty.

Spinning. The song of the spinning wheel by an open fire or by a cozy, old-fashioned kitchen range — who knows it today? Now slow ... now fast ... spinning ... spinning ... threads of this size and that. Heavy thread for heavy useful socks. Light, soft thread for baby things. Firm, narrow thread to weave cloth with.

Spinning in the fall. Leaves falling outside and brushing the windows. The strange pitiful whispers of them as they fell! ... Spinning ... spinning. ... The lamentations of cold winter winds. The barely audible song of falling snow, that, like a white fleece, lovingly and protectively covered fields and orchards, giving warmth and life to the kernels of buried winter wheat, to the green grass to come, to the saplings and old trees, to the berries and fruits of the next year.

Then the weaving. I shall always remember the big workroom of our sprawling house, with its big beams, from which hung golden chains of drying onions, bunches of sweet-smelling herbs, and long necklaces of finely cut apples and pears.

It was a big room. But the three looms took most of its space. There was the wool loom, on which woolen cloth was woven; the linen loom, for the fine linen threads, that became, under nimble fingers, sheets, towels, pillowcases, and dress lengths; and the rag loom, on which were made the long and short scatter rugs of many colors, so dear to the Russian housewife's heart, and for which she saved every scrap of material she handled through the year.

With a big work-cutting-out table, two sewing machines, and a big ikon of the Virgin Mother, the patroness of housewives and housework (before which a vigil light always burned), the room had an air of regal peace, and grave tranquillity which I have never felt or experienced anywhere else. It was a busy room. A prayerful room. Today I would say that its motto most assuredly was *Ora et Labora*.

I never quite mastered the art of "setting a loom" — of getting all the strands and threads that form the warp of the cloth into a pattern. I still have hopes. I know all about the woof, or crosswise threads that form the body of the cloth, for in my childhood, while Mother or some other experienced woman would "set the warp," I would be allowed to weave the cross threads with a big wooden shuttle. Now I would be given a small piece to do, now a bigger one. The day I was allowed to do a whole length of cloth for *my* own dress was, and still remains, a star-bright day for me.

But before weaving could be started, there was yet the dyeing to do. That meant going back to the herbs, roots, and flowers that we had gathered. It led us to the attic, where, on orderly shelves, Mother kept her herbal treasures, in jars, pots, and linen bags; a collection that, I suspect, would today be envied by collectors of such things.

She would sort out the proper ones, and then off we'd go to the summer kitchen. We did not have to be careful of this kitchen, the floors and walls were forever spattered anyhow, with the weirdest assortments of color dabs ever seen — reminders of preserves and jam-making.

For hours the pounding, grinding, mixing, and boiling of herbs would go on. Talk of witches' brews! In the steamy air, with our immense aprons and gay kerchiefs, Mother and I and the women helping us most assuredly looked like a group of Halloween witches who had lost their broomsticks.

Oh, but the end result of all this pounding and brewing!

I only wish that I could show my sophisticated modern friends the colors that came out of it all. The blues that I have never since seen duplicated; the delicate tones of it — the deep, glowing tints of it. The reds! From a vivid blood red, they ranged, to the gentle, soft colors of autumn maple leaves. The yellows. They glinted like gold, or spoke of spring and daffodils. The black had a sheen to it. The dark browns absorbed light and gave it back, changed. There were purples that made you think of Lent and penance; soft shades of violet that brought that humble flower right into the room, and lilac shades you could almost smell!

There they all were in the attic. Standing in bottles and flasks. A palette of colors an artist would envy. Ready to give their beauty to soft, white, hand-spun strands of wool, linen, or cotton.

The art of weaving linen is hard to master, the thousand-strand warp, hard to set. The knack of weaving in the woof, yet never missing one of the fine alternate threads — this requires years to get.

I am always fascinated by the miracle of transforming the lovely flax plant, with its blue flower, into yards of wide or narrow linens, that become heirlooms to be cherished from generation to generation and call to every woman to beautify them further with embroidery, lace, or drawn-thread work. I am fascinated, but, alas, I have never mastered it.

I learned many ways of embroidering and enhancing the beauty of linens. My mother taught me. She was a great lover of this Russian art. We would always seek new ways and new patterns from the village women we visited. Once, I remember, Mother was entranced watching a young woman embroider a linen towel, wide and well woven, with a scene of a rustic field full of flowers. Vainly she looked for a pattern. Finally she asked the woman for it. The latter smiled and pointed to the window before which she was working. There was the pattern, the field, full of summer flowers, waving gently in the breeze. . . .

The Russians may not have had marvelous indoor plumbing, nor thousands of laborsaving devices. But they had something more precious, which can perhaps be defined only as culture.

I wish now I had all Mother's recipes for making color out of plants, roots, and flowers. I have a few, but not nearly enough. If I had, I think I could brighten our gray, drab, colorless world with them, and bring to many people the knowledge and blessing of working with their hands . . . to produce beauty . . . which brings song and laughter. . . .

To weave a piece of cloth from one's own wool, or a sheet from one's own grown flax, or a rug from the leftovers of both — and to give the cloth the color that came directly from God! Then to enhance the piece further with the artist's touch of embroidery or lace! That is to know, in full, the words of the Psalmist:

"Let the glorious beauty of the Lord our God be upon us . . . and direct Thou the works of our hands. . . . Yea, the works of our hands do Thou direct. . . ."

Chapter Seven

THE FULNESS THEREOF ...

RECENTLY I saw in one of the slick magazines that cater to the "upper middle-class" housewife a series of pictures intended to make us realize how fortunate we are, we women of today, because we do not have to live "in the good old days" that knew not electric gadgets.

The article was illustrated to show the "differences" between those times and these. It was well done, photographically; and, to anyone unfamiliar with the past, very gratifying. For, quite evidently, the housewife of days gone by did not have any leisure at all — that is, according to the author.

As I read the article and surveyed the pictures, my mind went back to my Russian yesterdays, to a house far from any railroad, far from *groceterias* or food marts, far from all electric gadgets.

The matter of growing and preserving foodstuff was of grave importance. It was hard work too. But there was a strange deep feeling of satisfaction when it was all done. And there was more. There was a realization of a oneness with Nature and with God.

Somehow, I thought, this was the way He must have wanted us to live. It was good and right before His face. It united the family. It taught each member of it to depend utterly on God. It nurtured the virtue of trust and gratefulness in and to the Creator of all things, and it made prayer life the natural life of the family group.

At this home, gathering and preserving time started in an orderly fashion, early in the season, usually right after Easter. Mother and the cook and I would begin a systematic checking-up on last year's supplies. Armed with a pencil and paper, I would follow the two from attic to cellar, from the cheese and butter room to the vegetable dugouts, or root cellars, noting and jotting down the jars of this on hand, the bags of that, the pounds of this, and the quantity of the next thing, until hours later. Then the picture of what was there, and what had to be added, was as clear as day to the three of us.

The next move was a trip to the village store — there was only one — to get supplies of sugar, coarse and fine salt, and heavy needles. Then home again, to begin cleaning and scrubbing out the big brass bowls in which jams and preserves would be made, also to clean all the oaken barrels and the round white pine tubs. This done, all was ready to meet the spring, summer, and fall preserving of

The Fulness Thereof . . .

various foodstuffs, which included homemade wines and vinegars.

Spring, and dandelions making the fields a riot of glad yellow! Dandelion wine came first. What fun it was to gather the heads of the bright yellow flowers! Whole bags full of them! I helped clean them, and they had to be rinsed a hundred times or so — it seemed — to get the grit out of them. Then they had to be crushed and placed in boiling water — one gallon of dandelions — one gallon of water.

Three days they would remain drowned, with someone stirring them often. On the fourth day they would be squeezed dry and thrown out. The liquid would be boiled with sugar, orange and lemon rind (to each gallon of liquid, 3 pounds of sugar, the rind of one orange, and one lemon, with the meat of both thinly sliced and added), and let cool.

Then big fat chunks of bread would be toasted, spread with yeast cakes, and allowed to float on top of the liquid for six days to ferment it. Then the wine would be bottled, corked, and labeled. Rows and rows of bottled sunshine! And how the guests enjoyed this lovely wine, so easy to make, and so potent.

We had a special wine cellar where the temperature was always even. Through the seasons we made all kinds of wines. Apple, beetroot, red and black currant, elderberry, cherry, bramble, celery, carrot, rhubarb, prune, walnut, and vine-leaf wines. The neighbors vied with one another as to the quality and the potency of these products.

The North American Continent has made millions rich through the manufacture of all kinds of "soft drinks." But I have yet to find a drink as refreshing and cooling as

Russian Kvass which we made out of rye bread or apples or berries.

Some day, maybe, I will sell the recipe for this for a huge sum of money — which will go to help the thousands of friends of Friendship House who come to us for help. In the meantime, I will gladly give it to anyone interested "for free."

Though easy to make, wines were listed in our household as "extra" items. In preserving the main accent was always on foodstuffs. Berries, fruits, and vegetables made up the bulk of it. Jam was a big item, for Russians eat it with their tea. And they have tea almost all day long, but, officially, at least, five times a day — for breakfast, the noon dinner, at four o'clock, for supper, and then for the evening collation.

Tea-making is an institution and an art in Russia. Its center is the celebrated samovar. This is an all-Russian invention, consisting of a large urnlike contraption standing on a base. In its belly it has a funnel that widens at the base and into which live charcoal is placed. This heats the water in the urn to a boil, and keeps it that way for a long time.

The art of samovar-making was mostly reserved to the great city of Toula, and an art it most certainly was. We had brass, copper, silver, and even gold-inlaid samovars. But the majority had brass ones. At mealtime the boiling samovar was placed at the housewife's side of the table. Big vividly decorated china teapots were placed by its side. The mother of the family would then "make the teapot warm" by pouring some of the boiling water into it and then letting it run out into a basin that matched the teapot.

Then the good black tea, that came to us across the

The Fulness Thereof . . .

thousand miles from China, was carefully measured, one teaspoon for four cups, and again boiling water poured. The teapot was then placed over the samovar's funnel, that had a special place made for it. Three minutes, never a second more, and the tea was "brewed" and ready to pour into cups for ladies and glasses for men. No cream or milk spoiled its precious fragrance, but thinly sliced lemon brought it out. By the side of every glass or cup, there was a little dainty plate that matched the tea set and was known as a jam plate.

On the table a variety of jams offered themselves for selection. You took a helping of the one you liked onto the little jam plate, then put a spoonful of it into your mouth and drank a sip of tea. No sugar was needed.

So jam was a *big* item in any household. We, in ours, because of much entertaining, made about five hundred pounds of it each year, and there was seldom any left over for the next season. Jams were always made out of equal quantities of sugar and fruit or berries. Their variety was infinite, and a list of them would make a small book for sure.

It included delicate apricots, often mixed with ginger, quince, and oranges. Yet quince came by itself in a clear, gemlike syrup. And oranges in a thousand varieties produced marmalades and jams that shone in the sun in a real rainbow of gold and yellows. Apple butter, fragrant with spice, had a place of honor on the table too. Strawberries and raspberries were everyone's favorites.

True, such quantities of jams took miles of shelving. But where is the housewife whose heart would not rejoice at the sight of well-polished, neatly labeled shelves of beautiful, clear, fragrant jams? Ours definitely did.

Preserves, as known in America, were the exception in

Russian households, for the well-known Mason jars, or sealers, had not yet been imported. But special delicacies, such as tiny sweet-tasting peas, asparagus tips, and tomatoes, were packed in plain jars tightly sealed with wax.

The rest of the vegetables were dried — dehydrated — mostly sun-dried, but often, too, oven-dried. This latter was the simpler method, for every Russian farm boasted a bread oven; and everyone knows that these ovens keep just the right kind of drying temperature for a long time after the loaves are removed.

So the special vegetable pantry was filled year after year with hundred-pound bags of freshly dried beans, plain and lima ones, and peas. Large tin bins held diced carrots and parsnips, as well as Swiss chard, celery, and spinach all dried, for all these could be used for the favorite dish of Russia, soups, as well as for vegetable side dishes. The same pantry held well-labeled crocks of every conceivable culinary herb that could be grown locally, for Russians loved their cookies spiced with them.

Onions, garlic, corncobs were hung on old rafters in the kitchen, workrooms, and attic of the house in big decorative necklaces. Apples and pears cut up in even, round pieces and strung up with a heavy needle and our own linen threads, to be slowly dried in the sun only through the summer days, had a special place of honor. One corner of the attic was given over to them, where, in their exclusiveness, they could not be contaminated by any other odor.

Some berries were dried, too, as were some flowers. Wild raspberries and strawberries and the flowers of the camomile plant had priority, for they were used for medicinal purposes. If you ever have a high fever with a cold, make an infusion, or tea, of either of these two berries — a tablespoon to a cup of boiling water. Let it steep for ten minutes and then drink it, and watch your fever vanish in a sea of perspiration. Tastes good too!

Of course, besides pantries for jams, preserves, dried fruit, herbs, and vegetables, every country house had a root cellar, so constructed as to keep a portion of carrots, parsnips, turnips, beets, pumpkins and squash fresh and good to eat all winter. Sauerkraut, made in large quantities, was kept in special barrels outdoors, for freezing weather does not harm it.

Homemade cheeses of all kinds were stored in their proper places. They were made several times a year, so that matured supplies would always be on hand. Butter, of course, was made weekly; for we kept cows milking all the year around.

Potatoes had their own potato cellar, for there was a great mass of them — too many to store anywhere else.

Grains, like barley, oats, millet (used, alas, in the United States and Canada to feed fowl and canaries only), and buckwheat were kept in the flour house. And their gathering, milling, and storing was the job of the menfolks of the house. Russians eat buckwheat mostly in the shape of porridges. Oatmeal is used for breadmaking once in a while, and barley sometimes goes into soups to make them thicker and more nourishing. Sometime, you should try millet or buckwheat porridge — indeed you should, for your supper or breakfast — it tastes so good! Just take a cupful of either, cover with boiling water with an inch over, salt to taste, put into your oven, letting it "bake" for 20 to 30 minutes. Serve piping hot with butter and cream or milk. You most assuredly will find a new taste thrill on your table.

Whenever I think of early winter, and Mother inviting me to make the final tour of our "preserving" domain, I think of the Lesson from the Book of Wisdom: *Who shall find a valiant woman? The price of her is as of things brought from afar. . . . She has sought wool and flax and hath wrought by the counsel of her hands. . . . She shall not fear for her house in the cold snow. . . . Give her of the fruit of her hands, and let her works praise her at the gates. . . .*

Maybe the slick magazine I had been recently reading was right in many ways . . . but it left out so much. So much, that cannot be written or told or even photographed.

Chapter Eight

ON PILGRIMAGE

THEY all laughed hard. Not uncharitably, mind you, but lustily and joyously; and I really did not mind. Though, if the truth be told, I was confused because the cause of their laughter was myself. And yet, so far as I knew, I had done nothing funny, nor did I look unusual to myself.

For it was a pilgrimage, wasn't it? We all were to assemble at a given address, on that particular date, to go to the shrine of the Martyred Jesuits in Auriesville, New York. At least, that is what I had understood the day several weeks before when the little group I belonged to had discussed the last-minute plans.

Well, here I was, with my hobnailed boots, a knapsack, and a precious gourd of water. What was so funny about that? Yet they were laughing, a friendly, joyous, yet loud laughter. Finally one good soul exclaimed —

"Katie, you don't mean you thought we were *walking* to Auriesville! That's hundreds of miles away. We are going by bus, you nut...."

Well, well. It was, I confess, my turn to look astonished, and finally to laugh. By bus! A pilgrimage by bus! I had never heard of such a thing. And in my lifetime I had made many pilgrimages.

A pilgrimage was a sort of prayer: an act of penance, thanksgiving, or praise. How all this could be accomplished in a short bus ride was more than I could figure out. But then I was in America and not in Russia. When in Rome do as the Romans do. I climbed meekly into the bus.

As we rolled through a beautiful countryside, I was back in the soft pastel-shaded summer of northern Russia.

Soon the Little Lent would come around, the four weeks preceding the feast of SS. Peter and Paul, a time for fasting and penance. And as sure as not, Mother would begin first to think and to talk about, and then to prepare for, another pilgrimage to some holy place. She loved pilgrimages, especially to one of the many shrines of our Blessed Lady with which Russia abounded.

First, of course, one prays and reads up on the shrine one goes to. Let me see. From a bolt of clean, unbleached linen, made at home out of our own flax, one cuts the pilgrim's dress. A simple affair for women. Just a sort of kimono pattern. A hole for the head, and sleeves cut on the kimono style. Then one sews it with clean linen thread and a prayer. Now a linen cord, hand woven, and a linen sack, sewn neatly together and just big enough to hold a loaf of freshly baked rye bread, and a goodly pinch of rough salt wrapped in a clean linen rag. Clean and air the water gourd . . . and all is ready.

The morning of the pilgrimage is usually clear and sunny. It always was for us anyhow. Mass and Communion at the little country church. A light breakfast. No one eats much on penitential pilgrimages. Now the dressing, in the neat, clean garments prepared beforehand. The linen robe. The linen cord. A simple, modest, and easy-to-put-on attire.

Easy to walk in, too. We go barefooted. The bread and the water —. Now we are ready.

The family walks with us to the village green. Here the rest of the pilgrims are assembling, all dressed alike. All are barefooted. They may be, and sometimes are, princesses and dukes or peasants and paupers. But no one can tell which is which. The men wear linen trousers, a clean linen shirt.

The leader carries holy water. Now all kneel and ask God's blessing on the pilgrimage, and invoke the Angel Raphael, St. Joseph, and the Blessed Mother to be at their side through the journey. For they know all about traveling, don't they? Raphael was Tobias' guide, and the others made the journey afoot to Egypt.

Now the leader sprinkles all with holy water, and we are off. Relatives, friends, and onlookers speed us on our way, shouting their last demands for our prayers and intentions.

We have formed ourselves in a long straight line. The village is left behind. We start chanting the litanies — we will keep that up at regular intervals all through the journey. In between the litanies there is a great silence, in which each talks to God in his own way.

The road is soft under our bare feet. The flowers smell sweet. The clouds are white and gay in the blue sky. The forests we pass are cool and gentle, and a wind is on our sunburned faces. At times it seemed to me that all the world re-echoes the song of our litanies:

>Hail Mary, Mother of God, Virgin and Mother. Morning Star. Perfect Vessel.
>Hail Mary, Mother of God. Holy Temple in which God Himself was conceived.
>Hail Mary, Mother of God. Chaste and pure dove.
>Hail Mary, Mother of God. Ever effulgent light; from thee proceedeth the Sun of Justice.
>Hail Mary, Mother of God. Thou didst enclose in thy sacred womb the One who cannot be encompassed.
>Hail Mary, Mother of God. With the shepherds we sing the praise of God, and with the angels the song of thanksgiving. Glory to God in the highest and peace to men of good will.
>Hail Mary, Mother of God. Through thee came to us the Conqueror and the triumphant Vanquisher of hell.
>Hail Mary, Mother of God. Through thee blossoms the splendor of the Resurrection.
>Hail Mary, Mother of God. Thou hast saved every faithful Christian.
>Hail Mary, Mother of God. Who can praise thee worthily, O glorious virgin?
>*We salute thee, Mother of God....*

Yes, I am sure the earth sang with us . . . or maybe it listened.

Noon would come. The leader would call a halt, always by a clear river or stream. We would refill our gourds, wash our tired, hot feet, face, and hands. Pray and sit down to a lunch of rye bread, salt, and water. And did it taste good! Nothing ever tasted quite so good since. An hour's rest. A nap, and again a prayer. Holy water sprinkled on our rested brows . . . and off for the next lap.

Slowly we moved. Chanting. Slowly the day moved. Listening. And dusk was around the corner. Now we were near a village again. Thus it was planned. We were meeting people coming back from the fields and a day's work. All greeted us gladly and asked for prayers.

Now we were in the village. We broke ranks, and with a last injunction to be ready early and on the road, we made our ways to the little log houses, *isbas*, we call them in Russia. Now each person, or family representative, was knocking at a door, repeating the age-old formula:

"In the name of the Father, the Son and the Holy Ghost — we are pilgrims to holy places . . . begging for food and a night's lodging . . . in the name of God."

Invariably, the door would open, and hospitably we would be asked in.

"In the name of the Holy Trinity, come in pilgrims. Honor our poor house, and share with us what God in His great mercy has seen fit to send us today."

In we went, bowing low three times before the holy images and the Crucifix that used to adorn each Russian house . . . a bow for each Person of the Most Holy Trinity. Then the last and fourth bow to the hosts.

Now we were ready to wash up and eat. Whatever there was on the table was shared equally with us. All one poor family had to give us was bread, salt, and tea. The loaf was justly and accurately divided among the seven members of the family and my mother and me. We dipped the bread in the salt and drank the tea, realizing that we were immensely privileged, for we were seeing charity at its best — real Christ's charity — the poor feeding pilgrim travelers, because He was once One.

At night we slept in sweet-smelling haylofts. At sunup

we rose. Then a wash at the pump. A hastily drunk glass of cool milk. A piece of bread. A grateful farewell to our kindly hosts, with a promise to bring some sacramental from the holy place, and we would not forget. We were off again.

Days passed like the beads of a rosary. Slowly, reverently. In walking . . . close to God and the earth He made. In praying, begging . . . walking . . . resting . . . and praying again. Praying for our sins . . . for the world . . . for those we love. Just praying, praising, thanking God.

And then one day we would come to the shrine. Oh the joy of it! We had been walking a long time. We sort of knew that thus it would be when we would at last die in the Lord, after the long, tiresome journey of life. Just like now — standing on some knoll — seeing as yet from afar the spires of the holy shrine. Blessed be God . . . and His holy Mother!

Days, perhaps a week at the shrine. Living in the big monastery hostels built for the like of us. Having monks wait on us, silent and kindly. Visiting the shrine and the churches around it. Taking back a supply of holy oil, holy water, pictures, medals for those we promised to bring them to.

Masses, Matins and Lauds, the Little Hours, Vespers, Compline, in big, holy, beautiful churches. Praying and singing with the monks and nuns of near-by convents and monasteries. Several Masses a day — the glory of it! The joy of it! Like heaven or, at least, its hallway.

And then the way back, just as we came. The same hosts — now old friends. The sharing of gifts. The talking about God and the things of God.

And finally home. Sunburned. Healthy. Leaner. Filled to the brim in soul.

Yes . . . my yesterdays have great gifts for me. . . .

The bus lurched. Someone laughed. Someone passed me a sandwich and a Thermos bottle filled with hot coffee. In the back of the bus someone started to sing "Mairzy dotes."

My hobnail boots were heavy on my feet . . . my knapsack heavy on my lap. And I could not tell why — or could I? My heart was heavy with a strange sorrow.

Maybe it was just homesickness.

Chapter Nine

CHRISTMAS IN OLD RUSSIA

THE shops and emporiums of Chicago's State Street were dazzling in their array of lights and decorations. The crowds, dense and compact, seemed to be just milling around, content in savoring these early signs of their first postwar Christmas.

Above the din and noise of traffic rose the traditional songs and hymns of the season.

Feeling tired, both from shopping and from the crowds, I found a table in a quiet restaurant and was drinking a refreshing cup of tea. Then, suddenly, as has happened so often recently, the moment merged into my yesterdays.

Christmas in Old Russia

Christmas in Russia was the beginning and the end.

It was the end of waiting, and the beginning of a new year, for the liturgical cycle was part of the fabric of our living. The starting of expectation . . . of the coming of the Lord . . . the beginning of preparation.

My mother used to say that the days of Advent were the days of building a golden stairway that would bring us to a star, the star of Bethlehem, that in turn would bring us straight to the Christ Child!

To my youth that stairway was real. Each day I could see and touch each step of it, as it was being built. The first steps were made of cleanliness. We began *cleaning* from inside out.

First there was the Advent fast, to clean the soul of all past faults and sins, to make penance for them, to wash it with tears, and the heart with contrition.

Again, as in Lent, meat, milk, and all food made out of milk, eggs, or sugar disappeared from the family table, to be replaced with fish, vegetables, and honey. The Church again became the focal point of our daily lives, and Church services dominated the day.

But there was a difference. In Lent the Russian women donned dark garments, took off their jewelry, and allowed no music in the house for the forty, sad, cruel days of the Lord's Passion. Not so through Advent.

On the contrary, there was talk of new gay clothing, there was a flurry of buying materials and of sewing. There was much music in the air, and the practicing of hymns and songs to be sung on the Holy Night. Even the fast itself was one of joyous expectation.

Masses, Communions, confessions, and evening services in the church followed one another closely through the days. Christmas cleaning and scrubbing went on feverishly all about the house, with everyone humming snatches from ageless tunes.

First to be cleaned and polished were the ikons, which shone and became alive under the flickering shadows of the vigil lights — red and blue and green. To my childish eyes they were the forerunners of the lovely candles on the Christmas tree.

From the kitchen came strange spicy scents that could be smelled only at this time of the year. For a variety of cakes and cookies were being baked especially for Christmas.

There were, for instance, the gingerbreads, different in taste and shape from any other gingerbreads I have ever eaten. Some were cut in the shape of *the Lamb*, for wasn't Christ the Lamb of God? Others were made into big stars, for the Star of Bethlehem, and for Mary, God's Mother, the Star of the land and the sea. My favorite was made in the shape of a *Child in swaddling clothes*. . . .

Then, of course, there was the Christmas cake. Don't ask me what went into it. I could not remember. So much of so many things did. But what added to the anticipation of cutting and eating it were the little scrolls of paper that went into it — right into the batter, the dough of it.

On each piece of paper would be written the virtue one would have to practice through the coming year, for, definitely, one had to give the Infant Jesus a present, too, and everyone knows that all and each of the virtues were His most favored presents.

Interesting and fascinating as all the goodies cooked in the kitchen were, St. Nick topped them all. He was a mammoth gingerbread, all decked out with pink, green, and white decorations. Sometimes he was as big as a real baby.

Christmas in Old Russia 57

Everyone knows, of course, about St. Nicholas. For wasn't he commissioned by the Christ Child Himself and His darling mother and His good foster father, to come down to earth every Christmas, unto the end of time, to tell the children of all the world the story of the Holy Night, and to bring them gifts of the Holy Three — Faith, Hope, and Charity — and such other gifts as they in their littleness and simplicity desired, and had asked of the Holy Baby?

Only one St. Nick was baked in any household . . . for you had to be very good all through the year to get St. Nick. You worked hard for him all through the year. Yes siree, you certainly did! You had to be the best child in the family, the most deserving, to get St. Nick.

All through these weeks of preparation, like a conductor leading his orchestra, Father gathered the family, the servants included, nightly around the Advent wreath, and slowly, reverently read the Epistles and Gospels of the day weaving the old and the new, the end and the beginning, the Old Law and the New, into a chain of meditations and prayers that would hold all of us together for the rest of our mortal lives.

During the first week in Advent, one candle burned in the Advent wreath. Another was lighted as each week passed, until all four were glowing.

And then Christmas Eve! Starting with Church, continuing with a rigid fast that lasted until the first star! The grownups, behind closed doors, decorating the tree, making ready the gifts. The children huddling in corners and whispering in a fever of mounting excitement.

At long last the meager supper was over, and the last intolerable hours of waiting. Eight o'clock . . . and the sound of the tinkling bell of St. Nick!

We should have stampeded into the room of our dreams, the door of which was now opening slowly, but excitement rooted us all. We could hardly move.

Slowly the doors kept opening. On tiptoes we approached . . . *and here were Father and Mother . . . each holding the side of the door . . . opening it, opening it . . . until before our saucerlike eyes stood the Christmas tree, resplendent in its tinseled decorations . . . aglow with its myriad of colored wax candles . . . its stem draped in white and covered with synthetic snow that sparkled so . . . and all around it, parcels . . . each holding a child's dream. . . . Oh! the unforgettable ecstasy of that unforgettable moment.*

Still there was no rush. Mother and Father stood aside to let the children and the servants enter. Everyone did so decorously, and stood silently waiting for Father to read the Gospel story of the Nativity. Reverently he did. Then the whole household would break out into the natural song of all Christians . . . *Alleluia . . . Alleluia. . . . Glory to God on high and peace on earth to men of good will. . . . Alleluia . . . Alleluia.*

The singing over, Mother would start the distribution of presents, like mothers do all over the world, wherever Christmas is celebrated, bringing poignant joy to children's hearts. . . . For isn't Christmas the feast of Christ the Child . . . the feast of every *child* . . . and *doesn't the Word become flesh in every child . . . always?*

Now it was the children's turn to give the gifts of their hands . . . to Mother, and Father, then to each other, and to the servants. Now no one could find any order in this joyous disorder.

Finally satiated with excitement, all eyes turned to the table laden with food — nuts, candies, the Christmas cakes, and the virtues that we would offer the Infant, the gingerbreads, the spicy cookies, and finally the *big St. Nick*.

What fun to arrange all the animals and kings around the *Child in swaddling clothes . . . the Child that would be coddled and rocked to sleep by tiny loving hands all through the year to come. . . . Alleluia.*

Old and young . . . the living and the dead . . . all united in Christ the Lord on Christmas day in old Russia . . . the communion of saints becoming a reality of life. . . . Alleluia! . . . Alleluia!

State Street was ablaze with decorations and lights . . . the crowd dense and compact, the joyous hymns rising, rising above the noise and din of traffic. . . . Russia — my yesterdays . . . Chicago — my todays. . . . So different . . . so much the same.

A Child is born unto us, Alleluia, Alleluia! the Word was made flesh and dwelt amongst us. Alleluia.

Chapter Ten

EASTER IN OLD RUSSIA

THE evening service was over. The people were leaving. The church was dark again, with only the altar lamp and the vigil lights adding color to its dimness.

I was kneeling at the altar rail saying a few last prayers, the smell of incense heavy in my nostrils, when it seemed as if the church walls had dissolved and I was back again in the Russia of my forefathers . . . and it was Easter.

Easter in old Russia — the feast of feasts! More celebrated in that country than Christmas in the West.

To the Russian, who went to confession and Communion but four times a year at the most, Lent, the preparation for Easter, was a very holy, serious, and important time. It was a time of mourning, of cleansing, and of reparation, at all of which the Russian excels, as witness our literature with its deep analytical spirituality.

That is why, during the somber, tragic days of Lent, Russia became busy with nothing but the spiritual and the mystical. Life slowed down, became subdued. All ornaments were laid away.

During the first and fourth weeks and Holy Week, all public amusements ceased. Theaters, and such movies as there were, closed their doors. Even business made way for spiritual needs and practices, for the services during Lent were many and long. Offices, homes, and factories speedily adjusted their business hours, making special allowances for church attendance by their employees during the working day.

The fast was rigid, permitting no meat at all through the forty days. Fish was used on Sundays and a few weekdays, but not on Wednesdays, Fridays, or Saturdays.

In penance, prayer, and fasting, the Russian Lent passed slowly, mournfully. Holy Week drew near. Throughout Russia the atmosphere grew tense. Business stood almost at a standstill. All thoughts were with the Lord — in His Passion and in His Crucifixion.

Yet among all these spiritual exercises, every free minute was used for the physical preparations for the great day of the Resurrection. Not content with the cleaning done during the week of preparation for Holy Communion, all Russia washed and scrubbed and cleaned feverishly, for everything had to be resplendent for the joyous day of days, Easter.

The kitchen, too, teemed with activity. For Easter, food was very special, and it had to be cooked ahead of time. The *koolich*, a special rich bread, needed a lot of kneading and working at. I should like to meet the foreigner who could enumerate the ingredients that went into its making! And no matter how rich a family might be, how many servants it might employ, each member took a hand. Mother supervised the cooking, Father helped with the kneading, Sister shelled the almonds, Brother cleaned the raisins. All happy, flushed, and excited.

And the *paska* — what is it? I wonder. Cottage cheese, sugar, butter, eggs, all beaten and thoroughly mixed together by every hand in the family until it was a creamy white delicious whole. Then the mass was put in a special mold and under a heavy pressure, from which it emerged, days later, firm, about eight to ten inches high, with a cross clearly etched on each of its four sides and the letters *IX* (Jesus Christ in Greek) interwoven in it.

Then, oh joy, eggs were dyed. All the children, even baby, took part in this. Yellow, green, red, gold, silver, they were the first notes of color in the grayness of Lent, the forerunners of joy and spring — and of Easter and the Resurrection, Alleluia!

Yet all during these activities involving foodstuffs, not once was the fast broken. Impossible as it may seem, it was true. Although I must admit that the heavenly smell of a koolich baking is almost more than a person can bear, yet such is the strength of faith and custom that I never have heard of anyone's succumbing to temptation.

Holy Thursday. Memories of long ago. In the evening, the family went in a body to church. Each person carried a slender wax candle. This would be lighted during the long three-hour service of the "Forty Gospels," when the

Easter in Old Russia

life of Christ was read. Then everyone went home shielding the candle from the wind, for it had to be brought safely back, to light the perpetual fire burning before the ikon of our Holy Mother.

Many a Russian artist has rendered that home-coming of Holy Thursday night. The dark streets, the shadowy figures coming out of church, the lighted candles shielded by their hands, the light reflected on faces, old and young. A beautiful scene, worthy of the best talent, yet hard to paint because of the expressions on those faces.

For how can men paint God glimpsed in the faces of other men?

Good Friday. God is dying. It seems as if Russia died then too. Business closed down completely. No hustle or bustle in the streets. A hushed silence fell over the country. Government buildings were decorated in violet and black, the colors of mourning.

Only the churches were full to overflowing. In the middle of each stood a silver coffin surrounded by flowers offered by the faithful, symbolizing the death of the Saviour. An orderly, endless procession of people entered, approached the coffin, knelt, and kissed the cross on its sides. Princesses, chambermaids, workingmen, and courtly officers all mingled in the greatest democracy of all — that of Christianity.

At last Holy Saturday. This was also a day of fasting that would end only at midnight, which in old Russia was considered the hour of the Resurrection. But the fast could not suppress the air of great expectancy, nor take the glow of happiness from human faces. From ten at night until midnight multitudes, dressed now in the gay colors so beloved by the Russian peasants, or in their best finery, made their way to the churches.

The midnight Mass started at last. It began with the antiphon of Lauds for that day. In a loud, penetrating voice, the priest proclaimed: *Christ is risen!* The whole congregation answered: *Truly, He is risen.* Then the priest, turning around, kissed the deacon, who then passed the kiss of peace down the clerical line.

At this point a Westerner would have been sorely puzzled, for everyone in the church turned around and kissed his neighbor, exchanging over and over again the joyous salutation of the priest: Christ is risen! Truly, He is risen!

At that moment all the church bells started ringing freely, with a song of great gladness as if repeating, "Yes, Christ is risen! Rejoice all ye faithful! Love has conquered death! Christ is risen! Truly, He is risen!"

Beautiful and unforgettable was the sound of the "forty times forty" bells of Moscow. A boastful historian once said that they could be heard beyond the seas. I wondered. Could they? All I knew was that they echoed in every Russian heart, no matter where he was, at Eastertime, bringing joy and gladness even to exiles.

The service over, one more task was left: that of securing for the paska and koolich and eggs, that had been left in the sacristy, a special blessing. Then home through the illuminated streets. A jubilant town, filled with multicolored, hungry throngs, singing, kissing each other, wishing each other "Happy Easter," and hurrying home to eat, at long last, to repletion.

And at home all was ready. The house was clean and full of flowers, with a big table set in the middle of the dining room, the koolich in the center of it with two paskas at each side. Further down the table were the multicolored eggs, then the roast turkeys, chickens, hams, the wine, the fruit, the candies. Food enough for three days of rest and rejoicing!

And the presents were lying there too, for, in Russia, Easter was present-giving time even more than Christmas.

And last, but not least, was the fun of seeing "big sister" blush and blush again as a score of young men, having formed a queue, were claiming the kiss of peace from her pretty lips. For, as you know, no one could refuse that kiss in Russia at Eastertime. So the only thing left for one was to wish she were young and bold and pretty and in Russia during that holy season. Easter was youth's time. So the elders laughed a lot, teased a little, and let it go at that.

Now Father would cut the koolich, the symbol of the Bread of Life — Christ. And then a scoop of the paska, which symbolized the Lamb led to the slaughter. Thus were blended the Old Testament and the New. Now an egg, the symbol of infinity, of life eternal. Mother, bowing low, passed the plate with these three to family, guests, and servants, for all were gathered at the festive board. With these foods the Russians broke their fast, for it was symbolic food — food that had had a liturgical blessing.

Yes, Easter was the feast of feasts, the day of days.

Someone was gently touching my shoulder and whispering that it was time to go. The church was being closed for the night. I looked around. It was all dark. The vigil lights were all out. Only the altar light glowed blood red against the darkness. The sexton was speaking to me. I arose and left for home — but only part of me got there.

The other part was listening to the "forty times forty" bells of Moscow, that, I knew now, really could be heard beyond the seas.

Chapter Eleven

WE PRAY

IN THE past few years two books were published by the Rev. Father Philip T. Weller. Volume I is a masterful translation of the sacramental and processional rites of the *Roman Ritual*. Volume III concerns itself with the manifold and various blessings of the Church.

The English of these two books is sheer poetry, and either could easily be used for endless meditations on the mercy and goodness of God, who walks with man throughout his whole life, blessing and loving him and his labors.

To me these two volumes are a great joy. For they bring

We Pray

back vividly my Russian yesterdays and the peace in which, by God's grace, they were spent.

They also bring infinite sadness, pain, and sorrow into my todays, because I see how many people spend their whole lives ignorant of the love that God, and His Spouse, the Church, bear them.

I lament the emptiness that surrounds them in so many ways and the assistance and the blessings that, in their ignorance, they miss! What deep and profound lessons all these prayers of the Church could bring them — to ease the terrific burden of these tragic days — if they but knew them!

Many of the prayers and blessings of the *Ritual* are as familiar to me as the Our Father or the Hail Mary.

In almost every chapter of this present book, I have spoken of prayer. I have even included some prayers, here and there. I think it would be fair and truthful to say that, in those yesterdays of mine, Russian lives were lived in the shadow of prayer.

Early as the sun was rising, in our house and in millions of houses throughout the land, men and women were arising from sleep. Their first glance was toward the ikon in the eastern corner of the bedroom, before which always burned a vigil light. Their first gesture was the sign of the cross.

Up, washed, the bed made, or other chores attended to, rich and poor stood straight before the same ikons and recited their morning prayers. This might be done privately or in a family group. Slowly and with feeling the hallowed words were uttered. With many bows and genuflections. Then and only then did the real day begin.

Grace before and after meals! Prayers over this work or that! I remember so well, neither Mother nor the cook would place a dish on the stove, or bread (or any baking) into the oven, without first making three times the sign of the cross over them.

At schools, in shops, and in many factories, work began with prayer. But besides praying, yet as part and parcel of it, went fasting. To the Slav mind, the two always go together.

Wednesdays, Fridays, and Saturdays were fast days for many Russians. Wednesdays and Fridays were fast days for almost all of us. So were the vigils of all major feast days. So were the three "Lents" — the four weeks preceding Advent, the big pre-Easter Lent, and the two weeks before the feast of SS. Peter and Paul in July.

Praying before any kind of sport or fun was common too. A swift little petition to St. Peter was made by the fisherman on holidays. Another might be made by a boy or a girl, that this important "date" or party, might go off well. Prayer was made before a journey and upon safe return. There was praying before childbirth and afterward. There was praying at deathbeds and at wakes.

There was praying during pilgrimages and before and after examens. Russians, I must repeat, used to go through life praying and fasting.

As for blessings — it seems to me, in retrospect, that my life was filled with them. They encompassed me always and made me feel safe.

Father used to say that no real Christian should ever be afraid of anything or anyone. For was he not, if he were in the state of grace, the temple of the most Holy Trinity? And wasn't the Blessed Mother there? For where the Trinity was, there Our Lady of the Trinity was sure to be. And naturally his patron saint would be within him too. He had to be, as did the Angel Guardian.

We Pray

Furthermore, a Christian had the right and the duty, when in danger or need, to call on all the heavenly spirits for help, to call on anyone or everyone in the Church Triumphant.

So, living, walking, breathing in such a glorious company, how could one be afraid of anything but *sin*? Sin alone had the tragic power of separating us from God and those who are God's. Sin alone had the power to bring real death. It had to be feared with a great fear.

But back to the "blessings." There were first the blessings of the parents, which children remembered best. We were blessed at the beginning of each school year. We were blessed when we were sent on a journey, and when we undertook any special work or task of importance. We were blessed at our engagements and before and after marriage. We were blessed in sickness and in health. Thus our youth was spent under the powerful and efficacious parental blessings.

Strong, therefore, was an understanding slowly and powerfully growing in the souls of youth, of the vocation of marriage and of parenthood. Deep was the affection, the respect, and the love of a child for his parents. How could it be otherwise, since so clearly they held their rights, responsibilities, duties, and obligations directly from God, through the most holy Sacrament of Matrimony?

Russian literature clearly reflects this whole idea. It shows too the immense power and potency of a parental "cursing." That does not mean the use of bawdy and sinful words but the deliberate, biblical "cursing" by a father or a mother of their offspring. Terrible and fearsome is that act to the Russian.

It is said that the head of a man cursed by his parents

will find no rest, either here or hereafter. And it must be so. For ugly and sinful must be the act or acts that bring such a calamity on anyone's head.

Besides parental "blessings," the life of Russians was filled with many blessings of the Church.

No one would live in an unblessed house. So all were blessed by priests. Seeds, harvests, orchards, fields, tools and implements, machinery and stock, wools, linens, looms, ikons, crucifixes, cakes, breads, eggs, ales, wines, fishing boats, flowers, mills, medicines, bandages for the sick, mountains, meadows, grains, cooking and burning oils — all were blessed over and over again.

People received their share too, from God and Church, through priests. Infants, brides, mothers of newborn children, the sick, the pilgrims, the general travelers, each had his own blessing.

Then there were "blessings against" — floods, rats and mice, worms, locusts, fire, and other calamities.

Sacramentals also played a great role in Russian lives. Each child at Baptism received a rather large, brass, silver, or golden cross on a chain, which he wore all his life.

Woe to the one who lost this cross!

The value set on that cross was well exemplified by an age-old custom. If two people exchanged their baptismal crosses, they became, by that act, brothers or sisters in Christ; and so, were closer to each other than blood brothers or sisters. Such an exchange was made often during wartime, when one would rescue another from the jaws of death. The rescued would ask for the favor of such an exchange, considering that the least he could do to repay such a favor was to become a brother in Christ of the rescuer, and spend the rest of his life *"loving him in the Lord greatly . . . and serving him in God . . . constantly."*

Ikons, medals, and other religious objects were deeply venerated both for those they represented and for the blessings that were upon them. They were "holy things," to be used reverently and lovingly.

But *holy water* — water blessed by God and Church — that was the most powerful sacramental! Few Russians would be without it. Where is the Russian who does not believe in its potency against the devil and all the powers of darkness, in sickness and in health? If there be such a Russian, he is not any sort of Christian.

I remember my mother almost dying from cholera. Given up by doctors, she was lying cold and bluish on the bed. When I came in, my father was kneeling at the bedside, deep in prayer. I joined him. Then he arose and took a phial of holy oil, produced by the olive trees of Gethsemani, which he and Mother had brought back from a pilgrimage. He began to anoint Mother, all the while praying.

She got well. Skeptics can say that she would have recovered anyhow. But, humbly, I would answer that the power of God is infinite, and His blessing even on inanimate things is most powerful, especially when used with faith and the simplicity of utter trust. It can, and has, performed miracles.

I thank God that my childhood and youth was spent in a home, and partially in a country, that still believed in the existence of the prince of darkness, and in hell. Hell and Satan were made vivid to me. I had a wholesome fear of both, and a determination to escape both. Because of that fear, I was led gently but surely to the love of God. One of the greatest tragedies of our times is that men have ceased to believe in the devil and hence to worry about him — the most powerful spirit and intellect after God.

Yes, holy water was a constant companion of the Russian of old in his life's journey. He used it "to bless himself to sleep," in times of trial and sickness, in times of joy, in storms (when two blessed candles would be lighted, and the holy water would be sprinkled through the house), and in temptations. Always there was this little bottle of holy water. One felt safe behind its blessed drops, and behind the sign of the cross that always went with it.

Blessings often went with processions, and there were, it seems, an endless litany of both in my Russian yesterdays. Processions and blessings of rivers and lakes on the feast of St. John the Baptist — when also the evening bonfires were blessed. Processions in time of famine, war, epidemics, or plagues. Processions against tempests, and for rain. Processions on the feast of the Assumption of Our Lady, when orchards and their fruits were blessed. Easter processions, and those of major holydays. Processions on All Souls' day — to the cemetery with lighted candles. Their chants and prayers still fill my soul with joy and gladness.

Churchgoing was rather habitual. Especially during all the little and big Lents many hours were spent there before and after Mass. Visits were as natural as breathing. Daily in the big dim churches, one could see many people praying . . . praying . . . praying . . . in the lights and shadows of the tapers that burned by the hundreds before the gem-encrusted ikons.

Sundays saw all the immense churches and the little shrines and chapels packed to overflowing. Confessions were lengthy and penances hard. But always there were long lines of penitents. On holydays, the scenes were repeated.

Yes . . . Russia prayed, did penance, and fasted much. It used, too, all the wealth and beauty of the Church's many ways of helping her earthly children to attain God's Kingdom of Love.

Is it to be wondered at that Our Lady of Fatima wants Russia to come all the way back home? What treasures of sorrow, pain, suffering, prayer, penance, fasting, and *love* she can bring to the world when she returns!

It may yet be that Russia will lead the world back to Christ some day. And soon. For she had lived in Him, in His Mother and His saints, and in the Holy Trinity, so many centuries!

Chapter Twelve

I TAKE THEE

THE affairs of the heart, as a Frenchman would say, were conducted in Russia much after the pattern of all Western Europe — with a little tinge of the East added.

Ah yes, the East! It must never be forgotten that for four hundred years, Russia had been engaged in wars and skirmishes with her conquerors, the Tartars.

Incidentally, she receives very little credit for this from the Western historians. They constantly seem to overlook the fact that, through those wars, Russia kept the invasion of the Mongols within her own borders, thus saving the West their devastating influence.

However, those four hundred years left their mark on the whole of Russian civilization and character. She absorbed some of the mores and customs of the Tartars, and, in a manner of speaking, Christianized them. But the legend is that Russia, and Russians, are mysterious, with the strange mystery of the East and a stranger mixture of East and West. Even to this day this baffles the Western observer, though he shrugs it off with the saying, "Scratch a Russian and you'll find a Tartar."

Like all other European nations, Russia guarded her daughters in the matter of social relations by means of duennas or chaperons. There was also a rather rigid code of behavior which, unless strictly observed, brought ostracism to the culprit.

Moreover, as they were deeply religious the people venerated purity, innocence, virginity. Men looking for a wife demanded these virtues. Being realists, they understood that "platonic relations" between the sexes were the figments of creative writers only. Furthermore, being firm believers in the Mystery of Iniquity, and of the Devil, and having a watchful attitude for the occasions of sin, Russian parents felt it their duty to guard and help their daughters. Human nature, corrupted by original sin, they believed, had to be safeguarded by the elders, especially in the days of its youth.

Thus it was that in the heart of Russia, its little hamlets, villages, and small towns, girls never ventured out alone into country roads or lanes. Their trysting place was either the home of the girl's parents or the village green, where parties and dances were held during suitable seasons, and where, on Sunday afternoons, it was permissible to walk in pairs or to have a picnic under the shady trees.

The village green usually stood in front of the church,

and could be seen from almost every house around; those houses in their neat, straight rows.

Should a maid disregard the age-old custom, she would probably die a spinster — for though male youth eagerly would walk the forbidden lanes with her, the mere fact that she had acquiesced placed her in the strange category of "girls one might walk with but never propose to."

In big cities and towns, and in the upper strata of society, the code was just as rigid, and enforced through the chaperonage of young girls either by an elderly female relative, her parents, or a hired chaperon-governess.

But love has her way always. Neither lock nor key, chaperons nor duennas have yet succeeded to thwart her. Thus, surrounded by obstacles unknown to the freer and easier ways of the North American Continent, Russian youth plunged into courtship that was both more adventuresome and more fun. At least, I think so.

Eventually, to each came that special *day* when *he* asked, and *she* answered with that tremulous *Yes!*

It may have been accomplished to the bars of a waltz, danced under the vigilant eyes of their elders, or during the split second when a square dance brought her into his arms. Who can tell? The question was asked — the answer given.

But "much can happen between the time a cup is lifted, and the time it reaches the lips," says an old Russian proverb. And often much did. For, it was not quite enough for her to say *Yes*. Her father and mother had to do likewise. That meant he had to ask them for her hand.

However, nine times out of ten, he heard the joyful verdict from the lips of her parents, which meant the realization of his great dream. Of course, while he was "asking" she would not be very far away. Probably she was hiding behind a half-opened door or a curtain.

Thus when her mother came to call her, she did not have far to go, for she would appear instantly, flushed and eager with shining eyes and a happy, shy smile. Mother understood and smiled, too, tolerantly. Hadn't she gone through the same thing years ago?

For a moment they were left alone while parents went to fetch the family ikon of the Blessed Mother from their bedroom. This was to be one of the few occasions when the ikon would be taken down.

Back into the living room the parents would come. The happy couple would kneel at their feet. The father, lifting the ikon high, would bless them, making the sign of the cross with it. The mother would repeat the sign and the formula.

A toast would then be drunk to the young people's happiness, and the engagement became semiofficial. The same ceremonies would be repeated a few days later at the house of the boy's parents.

However, the engagement would become fully official only after it received the blessing of the Church. For Russians firmly believed that when a man and woman pledged themselves to enter the great and holy Sacrament of Matrimony, that the in-between time, the time between the engagement and the wedding, must be given to God through a solemn ceremony originated by His holy Spouse, the Church.

The beautiful rite of betrothal can be found in that translation of the *Ritual* by Father Weller, mentioned at the beginning of this chapter. It is truly worth studying, reviving, and, above all, putting into practice on this continent of ours where engagements are entered into so easily and carelessly, and are broken so readily. It is this attitude, I think, that is responsible, to a great extent, for our irreverence toward the Sacrament of Marriage.

In Russia, the betrothal ceremony took place before an altar. The engagement and wedding rings were blessed, and both were placed on the third finger of the girl's left hand. After marriage the wedding ring would be worn on the right hand. Mass and Communion followed.

Thus was a solemn promise taken before God. It could not be lightly given, nor disregarded. Human hearts and souls are not playthings of lower passions or passing moments.

The ceremony was also legally binding. True it did not bind parties to marry under pain of mortal sin. But, nevertheless it was valid both before ecclesiastical and civil courts, especially in matters of inheritance.

Perhaps because of this serious and sacramental approach to engagements, it took me literally years to understand the ways of maid-and-man in the U.S.A. and Canada. For here was the utter reversal of everything I knew. It seemed that over here the girl who could boast of the most broken engagements was the most popular with the opposite sex and the envy of her own! Promises were but the breath of scented night air — and love, if *love* it was, seemed but a swift passing shadow, illusory in the moonlight, gone with the rising sun.

But, then again, I may have misunderstood. Maybe ... I was ... and am ... old fashioned.

Being engaged was fun. It always is — everywhere. In Russia, you, of course, saw quite a bit of *him*, yet still you were never quite by "yourself." Oh, you could, once in a while, go together to a show, a restaurant, a tearoom, or even to a dance with a crowd of friends. But you had to be circumspect and not stray from the allowed and beaten paths. Once in a while the family would leave you alone, for a few minutes, in the living room. But such moments were few and far between.

Engagements were short. It was felt that it was best to have them that way. For, again, one must guard against occasions of sin. Always. And long engagements surely led to such. Furthermore, what *was* the sense of a lengthy engagement anyway?

Of course, it may be argued, a young couple in love should wait to marry until such time as the husband-to-be is somewhat "established," with enough money to support a young wife and a growing family. In the West, alas, this also means that a certain "standard of living" must be maintained if the young couple really wants to "amount to something," be "successful" in the worldly sense of the word.

Somehow, that did not seem to matter too much in the old days in Russia. True, the ways of life were more stable. People "stayed put" longer. The land, farming it, living on it, was the accepted way of life of the majority. All of this contributed to ease the ways of the young folks. As likely as not, they would get a plot of land. They could build out of logs, there being an infinite acreage of virgin forests. The girl's folks would provide the dowry, such as it was, in household goods, chickens, a cow, maybe, or two. And, before you knew it, the young folks were farming on their own, with the rather primitive machinery and the old ways of their forefathers. City and quality folk followed the same pattern — the girl bringing to her marriage the bedding, napery, clothing, and often cash, and the groom providing the house furnishings and the apartment or the house or the room, as the case might be.

It was believed that youth should make their future together, accepting together the lean and the fat times, that in so doing they would be welded into one, both in flesh and spirit more completely than if all had been already provided before marriage.

By and large, the Russians did not care too much for worldly goods, savings, money, and the like. They were more interested in *being* than in *having*. Their whole spirituality bespeaks this trait, which was also reflected in their marriage and the preparation for it.

Hope chests were started with the birth of a girl. As she grew, she contributed much to it by the work of her hands. Home-woven and embroidered linens and other things of lasting beauty were carefully put away into beautifully carved hope chests. Yes, these hope chests really existed. Woolens were specially treated against moths and kept ready for use and for changing fashions. This, too, made it easier to start housekeeping.

Thus the great day of the wedding would dawn quickly for the engaged couple. And it was always a *great* day. Church weddings were a *must*, and all over the land. Gorgeous in their wonderful ceremonies and trappings, they remained indeed memorable for the couple and for their relatives and friends.

Mass and Communion usually followed the marriage ceremony. Parental and Church blessings came thick and fast throughout that hallowed day. The parents of the bride would hurry out of the church as soon as the ceremonies were over and rush home, so as to greet the newlywed pair at the door. The father would have a loaf of bread, held on a richly decorated wooden plate, over which was laid an intricately embroidered linen scarf. The mother would present the salt in a beautiful handmade dish.

The bread was to remind the young people of the natural life that bread sustained, and the supernatural life, of which it was so glorious a symbol. The salt was to remind them that they belonged to the Mystical Body of Christ, and hence they were the *salt of the earth* — the salt that must not lose its flavor.

Having presented the bread and salt, the parents, both sets if present, again blessed the couple with the family ikons, one of which was now presented to them for their keeping.

Later the bridal chamber was to be blessed by the priest. "Bless, O Lord," he would say, "this bridal chamber, that they who share it establish themselves in Thy peace and conform themselves to Thy will. And as their years increase, may they be enriched with the fullness of life, and finally come into Thy heavenly Kingdom. Through Christ our Lord. Amen."

There would follow the time of gaiety and rejoicing. Dancing, eating, and merrymaking would go on for three days and nights. It was usual for the bridal couple to participate, retiring to their blessed bridal chambers overnight, to rejoice with their friends on the morrow.

Of course, the wealthy and upper classes had adopted the Western-style honeymoon. But the custom was not too widespread. For the attitude to marriage, sex, and the like, was so interwoven with God and the Church that it carried easily its true aura of beauty and vocation to all who took part in its celebration. Begun with Christ, and in Him consummated! That was Russian marriage.

Is it to be wondered at that there was little confusion, in the minds of the Russians, as to the ends of marriage?

Reverently they looked on virginity, purity, and innocence in the young unmarried women. Reverently, too, they treated pregnant women. For motherhood *was one of the main ends of marriage*. It was the fruitfulness of love and the visible sign of God's choicest blessing on the union between man and woman.

Recently a visiting Eastern prince was asked his impression of American women. Politely he declared they were both charming and beautiful. But, he wondered, why were so few of them pregnant?

The remark was thought to be funny. But was it?

It seems strange to me that, on this side of the Atlantic, the blessed months of carrying a child should be camouflaged by skillfully designed clothes. As if there were something shameful in the prenatal carrying of a child.

"My dear, I would never have guessed! You do not show it at all." That seems to be the greatest compliment a pregnant woman can receive from her friends! Why? Is motherhood so hideous that it must not be seen? Is "pregnancy" a word never to be used in genteel company? Or is the body of a woman with child — the visible sign of an invisible grace — so ugly it must be concealed?

In my Russia and in most other parts of the world women were proud to show their motherhood-to-be to the whole world. That "world" loved and respected it greatly. And it showed this feeling in a thousand ways.

The visit or the passing-by of a woman with a child was always considered a blessing by my friends. Perhaps they remembered the visitation of our Blessed Mother to her cousin Elizabeth.

Large families were the rule and not the exception.

Artificial birth control was almost unknown. And if it was practiced in secret, those who practiced it definitely understood it to be a grave sin. There was, at least, no hypocrisy.

Perhaps, because of the "Eastern tinge," the heritage of Russians from their four hundred years of Mongol invasion, the woman was satisfied to be the queen of her home and the mother of many children. She had little or no ambition to shine in the political or the business world. Neither did she crave an existence full of excitement and change. *Home* was a real word to her. It meant so many inexpressible things. Safety. Peace. Happiness. The tranquillity of God's order.

Anyhow, that is how I remember my home.

Chapter Thirteen

MAY THE SOUL ...

DEATH was simple in my Russian yesterdays. There wasn't the fear that seems to shroud her or any mention of her in our modern days. Because she was the inevitable, people took time to consider her, to get acquainted with her, so to speak. They prepared themselves to meet her and to welcome her.

Outsiders often were heard to comment that the Russians were fatalists, and that the Eastern influences "that shaped the Russian character" were most assuredly at work here. They thought that *kismet*, the oriental word for "fate," which implies the impossibility of fighting it,

May the Soul . . .

and the need to morosely surrender oneself to it, was the set word of the Russians in the matter of dying. In other words we just said "kismet" and gave up the ghost!

But like many other preconceived notions, this bespoke the ignorance of the strangers within our gates.

The truth was far more simple, and much more beautiful than this rather rash and generalized statement. The truth was to be found in the intense faith of the people and their understanding of the most holy will of God.

In the Western Churches, pious folks are wont to recite this rather beautiful prayer of resignation: "My Lord God, even now I accept at Thy hands, cheerfully and willingly, with all its anxieties, pains, and sufferings, whatever kind of death it shall please Thee to be mine."

The Russians did not say any prayer on the subject — they just lived it from day to day, and did not forget that such a "living" necessitated a general and constant attitude of mind, soul, and heart. All these had to be always and continually exercised in submitting cheerfully to the most holy will of God, through one's whole life, to be ready to do so when death approached.

I remember one day when my father came into the house with a smile on his face and, handing Mother a lovely piece of jewelry, informed her that this would be his last token of love for quite a while, for he was utterly ruined, and that though we would have to drastically change our mode of living there was little to worry about for *"God had given and God had taken away. . . . May the most holy will of God be done in us. . . . Alleluia!"*

It was. It has always seemed to me that ours was the most cheerful "ruined" family I knew.

No. It was not oriental fatalism that filled Russian

souls. It was, rather, deep love and understanding of God's will and a simple conformity to it.

Many there were who earnestly and dutifully prepared themselves for death. I remember many holy pilgrims who used to stop at our house, discussing, beautifully and simply, their preparations for the day when death would come to lead them to Life.

They would tell of the many prayers for a Christian death they were saying. They would speak of the penances they were inflicting on themselves, of the long vigils devoted to these wholesome and holy thoughts. They went on to say how one should live, if he were to be ready to die in the Lord. I remember many of their stories. Maybe, someday, I will have time to write them. They would make wonderful, though perhaps somewhat startling, meditations for our confused world which has developed so thoroughly the cult of the body beautiful and neglected the nurturing of the beautiful soul.

In the villages around us, which I so often visited with my mother, bent on errands of mercy, or with my nurse — just to visit her folks and friends — we often would watch men fashioning their own coffins and weaving shrouds for themselves or for their kin.

The best flax, the smoothest wood, and the most skillful workmanship went into both.

Nor were the dead forgotten. Constant prayers sped up to heaven for their souls. Anniversaries were scrupulously observed, and in every Sunday Mass the dead were mentioned by name at the altar of God.

The Eastern liturgy differs somewhat from the Western. In our churches, the deacon, or reader, at the Memento of the Living, and again at the Memento of the Dead, would read names from the family books he

May the Soul . . .

kept. These "family books" were quite an institution. Some were plainly bound. Some were bound in silver and gold. But every family had them. They were divided clearly in two parts — *The Living* and *The Dead*.

Before Mass, the head of the family would peruse the book, which measured seldom more than six by four inches, and either leave it as it was or add a name in one part. The book was brought to the vestibule of the church, where a sacristan presided over a table. This table, was, by the way, filled with candles and unleavened breads. The faithful would select a loaf, and a taper, too, perhaps, and make an offering while handing in the books.

The loaves and the books were taken to the priest. He, with a little triangular golden knife, cut tiny triangular pieces out of the bread. These pieces would go into the chalice and be consecrated, as the Body of Christ.

In the Eastern Rite, Communion is given under two species.

Thus, you might say, the living and the dead shared in the Holy Sacrifice, through the offering of the faithful, as it was done in the days when the Church was young.

All Souls' Day was a major holyday in Russia, for the love of their dead was deep and abiding in the hearts of its people. Throughout the land, at Mass and in special prayers, the dead were remembered solemnly and with all the family present. All day the cemeteries were filled with throngs, praying, fixing graves, visiting the beloved who slept their last sleep.

At eventide, there were more prayers in the church and there was usually a candle procession to the cemetery, with everybody chanting litanies and hymns. The candles were left to burn on the graves, in little containers or lanterns. They made beautiful patterns of light and shadows for passers-by to see. They demanded that all who saw must whisper a prayer as they went by.

Praying as one passed a graveyard, any graveyard, anywhere in the land, was a "must" for a Russian. Men would life their hats respectfully, and both men and women would whisper a prayer that the souls of those resting in this cemetery might know the deep peace of a Christian's final rest.

To clean and adorn cemeteries was considered one of the corporal works of mercy, but to me it was a human joy too. For the Russian cemeteries were indeed fascinating. They sprawled unevenly, at least in the country, all around the Church.

Their wooden picket fences were often painted red, blue, or white. Some remained unpainted and acquired that gray, satiny paint that hardwood gets when exposed for a long time to rain, sun, and snow, with an undertone of faint violet or purple. I loved these fences ever so much better than the painted ones. Each grave had a wooden cross, surmounted with a little roof, that made a sort of shrine, under which an ikon might be placed, together with an enclosed lantern that would burn on big feast days in lieu of a vigil light.

Then the cemetery looked beautiful with its big trees and simple flowers becoming immense in the shadows thrown from the gently swaying lights.

Always there were special nooks and corners in every cemetery that attracted the passer-by to stop, rest a while, and say a prayer for the good souls that slept so peacefully in these homey surroundings. I remember especially a little corner by the huge lilac bushes that I could never resist. When they were in bloom their scent could be smelled afar off, the more so because at the feet of the lilac trees there was white carpet of lilies of the valley, Russia's favorite wild flower, of which there were so many in the woodland lots. I have never since smelled so sweet a fragrance as that of lilacs and lilies of the valley.

Spring and fall brought out the villagers to clean the cemeteries, rake the leaves, cut the dried branches of the many trees, and plant new flowers.

Besides cleaning the abode of the dead and the beautifying of them, the preparation of the body for a decent burial was another part of the same corporal work of mercy — *burying the dead.*

It was the privilege of the older women to attend to it, but always they brought some young ones with them, to teach them the reverent art of laying out the dead.

Litanies were recited during this last work of mercy that neighbors could render the deceased — litanies and long, lovely prayers for the dead. There was nothing frightening or distasteful in the performance, for every gesture was full of love and respect. And love makes all things right and proper.

Wakes were solemn affairs, much resembling the Irish wakes in this part of the world. The family, visiting pilgrims, nuns, and friends prayed constantly, in relays at the coffin. Not for one second was the body left alone or without prayers while it remained in the house.

Yes, death was simple in my Russian yesterdays. Simple, beautiful, sacred, to be made ready for by a life lived in conformity with God's most holy will.

Chapter Fourteen

VILLAGE LIFE

IT HAS always been hard for me to explain the real life, history, and background of Russia to anyone not conversant with them. It seemed always such a gigantic task. I knew I would have to start with the A B C's, and somehow that always seemed to baffle and amaze my hearers. So I usually faltered and sometimes became inarticulate. I never went beyond the very beginnings. For there was nothing to hook my stories onto. No one, it seemed, had studied Russian history or Russian geography. This latter in most minds was very hazy — compounded of ideas of vastness, of Siberia, stuck somewhere in the north, of intense cold, and of mountains of snow in which wolves prowled freely.

The pre-Communist way of life was another blurred picture full of strange and amazing facts and fancies — mostly fancies. Generalizations were the rule. The talk went something like this.

"The Russians were a backward people, illiterate and unhygienic. They lived under a reign of terror, the source of which was the Czar and his regime. They hadn't the faintest idea of any democratic processes. Life was bleak and spent in fighting the climate and the political odds!"

As I stated in my preface, this is not a book of Russian history, nor do I wish to enter into any controversies nor to raise any. All I want to do is to state certain facts that were part of the fabric of my own life, hoping that in a very small way I might shed some light on a nation that baffles so many experts today, and bewilders the average man on the street.

But especially is this little book of mine directed to my fellow Catholics; so that understanding the deep-seated faith in God that lives in the Russian soul, they may pray, with renewed fervor, for the ultimate conversion of Russia — dear and so close to the virgin Mother of God.

Russia was and, for that matter, still is, predominantly an agricultural nation. The nerve center of its life, therefore, was the village. Having spent much of my time in many villages, I always go back to them in my memories. They, rather than the big cities, show me the land of my forefathers.

Russian villages were most stable. Their structure was quite different from any such places elsewhere. Generations were born, brought up, and died in them. But their stability was also due to the way the land was divided among its inhabitants.

Each family, of course, owned its own plot. But in each village there was also a communal land, which was divided and redivided each spring, according to the number of people in each family.

Thus, should John, the elder son of farmer Ivanoff, get the wanderlust this year, and depart into the city to try his luck in a factory, or apprentice himself to a trade, he did not at once join the ranks of the proletariat or propertyless people. For back home there was always waiting for him a piece of the communal lands.

The Village Council would, every spring, gather together and count the heads of each family. So many sons had left this one, so many daughters had departed from that one. Hence these families would have so many less mouths to feed. Hence, too, they would need less of the communal land to till. So their plots could be redistributed, to give more acreage to others — to families whose sons had returned from their wanderings or who now had more children than they had before.

Thus it went. Every year a new pattern. Every year a just allotment.

Naturally, many sons never returned. Once it was definitely known that they had severed their connections with the village, their names were taken off the lists, and their shares henceforth were given to others.

It helped a lot to give background, a sense of "belonging" and of having something always to fall back upon, to those who went off to distant places. It also alleviated the tragedy of the city workers. If things didn't work out right, they could always go home and farm. This gave them time to find things out in the city and to

Village Life

evaluate their new lives before settling down for good.

It also resolved some of the problems now confronting the highly industrialized countries of the West, with their unmoored, propertyless proletariat that is prey to so many ills. Leo XIII and Pius XI would have loved this whole Russian idea!

But there was one shadow on this original and quite just way of life. That was the fact that the nobility had immense private holdings, which necessarily reduced the acreage that could be owned by peasants and villages. This fact, little known or understood, is in my estimation one of the reasons why Communism was so successful in a country to which it was utterly unadapted and unsuited. Its father, Karl Marx, meant it for the highly industrialized nations, not for almost completely agricultural Russia.

At the beginning of this century, the peasants were restless because their private holdings, as well as their communal ones, were too small adequately to feed an ever growing population. Realizing that their lives depended on satisfying the just needs of the agricultural millions, the nobility petitioned the Czar, around 1908–1910, to resurvey all of Russia and define their property lines clearly. Then they offered to sell to the government great parts of their holdings, at a very low price, to be turned over to the villages on long-term easy payments.

This suggestion was accepted. The resurveying of the immense country began. A decade would finish the work. But World War I intervened and stopped the surveying.

It was in the trenches, and as a nurse then, that I heard with my own ears the Communist propaganda directed at the soldier-peasants. It centered on *their private and communal ownership of the land.* The idea was that the soldiers should desert the army immediately, go back to their homes, and take over the lands of the nobles, killing them if need be.

Hunger for ownership, and the need of it, drove the Russian peasants in the army to do just that. For a year, two, or three, the peasants did own the land they had so brutally taken. But then the Communist government turned right around and *took all the land away from them,* making it all government land. The farmers were organized into collective farms, becoming but tenants on the lands they had so wanted. Tenants? Say, rather, they became slaves, working and existing under constant and strict supervision of the Communist government.

Only those who know the love and the hunger of the Russian peasant for his land and his primordial desire to own it personally and communally will understand that right there was sown the beginning of the end of Communism in Russia.

Patient, long-suffering, the peasant will bide his time. But when it arrives, he will come, in all his vast numbers, to the side that will guarantee him that ownership. Here, in the heart of the humble millions lies the key to the future overthrow of the existing regime.

But there was more to the village than just ownership of land. It was one of the most compact and closely knit human groups that ever could be found. To the eyes of a stranger it presented always the same structural pattern.

The church stood at the end of a neat row of houses that faced each other. It was shut off from them by a large piece of land that was called the village green. Its lawns rivaled some of the best in England.

This structural pattern was also a symbol of the deep

Village Life

spiritual life of the Russian peasant — which wholly centered around the church that so artistically dominated the landscape.

Each house had an individuality all its own. True, all the roofs were thatched, and most of the houses were built of huge logs, except in the southern part of Russia, where there were few trees and where the prairies or steppes stretched out their immense undulating acres as far as eyes could see. There the huts were made of mud and, being whitewashed at least four times a year, stood gleaming, dazzling white under their straw roofs.

Mud huts or log cabins, the houses were known as *isbas*, the Russian word for "cottages." Much of the skill and art of the owners went into the trimmings. Doors and window frames were beautifully carved and were often painted in vivid colors. Their many original designs were the envy of city artists.

The back yards were masses of flaming colors in the spring, summer, and autumn of the year, for Russians were both lovers of flowers and experts at gardening. The front yards, usually enclosed in artistically wrought fences, invariably sported long golden rows of sunflowers. The seeds of these, dried and boiled, took the place of peanuts for the children. Benches, laboriously carved, stood before each gate. Not being plagued by mosquitoes and black flies, folks sat cozily there at eventide, exchanging gossip and the news of the day.

Each house was usually reached via a few steps and a tiny veranda, and each veranda had an overhanging roof. The front door was painted in bright colors. It led into a cool hallway.

The majority of the houses, though, had just one big room. Dominating it was the oven. Russian ovens are their very own. I haven't seen the like of them anywhere else.

The oven occupied a goodly part of the room, and was made with bricks covered over with cement or clay. Into their front was bricked-in an ordinary wood-burning range, on which the cooking was done. Just back of the range was the bread oven. It rose almost to the ceiling. The top of it, and often the sides, which were made in a sort of wide stairway, the steps of which served as beds for the children or older members of the family who needed this heat in the cold winter nights.

In the eastern corner of the main room, there would be benches, nicely carved, fitting the corner. Before them would be a big table. The whole would be blessed by a series of ikons of our Lady, our Lord, and such saints as were special friends of the household.

Before them would burn one or two vigil lights encased in silver or copper holders on long chains, hand wrought. The walls around the ikons would be decorated with white linen towels, intricately embroidered in the Russian housewife's favorite cross-stitch, turning that corner into one of the most colorful parts of the room, and one of the most beloved and cherished.

The cooking utensils were mostly copper and iron, often handmade, and always highly polished. Pottery jugs, bowls, and plates, with many designs of varied colors, were used for everyday service, adding their artistic touch to daily life.

Beds were another witness to the many handicrafts of the Russian people. There was the hand-woven linen for sheets and pillowcases: many pillows, one on top of another, thrown over a much-embroidered counterpane; the carved wood of the bedstead. All this bespoke a love

Village Life

of beauty and an infinite patience in craftsmanship. There were villages in Russia that were known for their beautifully lacquered furniture, their black, red, and yellow designs. Others were famed for their painting on wood, though the artist used the patterns of folklore and imagination only. Some villages were skilled in copper and brass works, others in pottery and linen or embroidery and weaving or the making of toys.

Those arts, skills, and crafts were passed on from generation to generation, always perfected, always exhibiting originality and beauty. Even today, in the markets of the world, these original handmade things bring a high price.

Often, if the room were big enough, it would hold the weaving loom and the spinning wheels. Large wooden chests covered with intricate designs of brass and tin would contain the clothing of the family. Conspicuous, usually, were the lovely hope chests that held the slowly accumulating dowries of fine linen and clothing, handmade and worked all through the childhood and adolescence of the girls of the family.

Slowly the centuries-old pattern of days flowed through the village. Up at sunrise, to pray together — then off to the fields went the menfolks, while the women took up the round of household and farm chores. All through the working seasons lunch was brought to the men in the fields. Thus the main meal was usually the evening supper, eaten around five-thirty o'clock.

Often have I heard doctors and dentists exclaim about the teeth of Russian and Central European people, and wish that the Western nations, whose children and adults had such poor teeth, would adopt the diet of my people! This always makes me smile. For I cannot quite picture

Canadians or Americans, used to soft, precooked, prepared foods, wrestling with the diet of Russian peasants!

Take breakfast, for instance. As often as not it consisted of sour milk or cottage cheese, eaten with big chunks of rye bread made of coarsely milled grain and smeared with freshly churned butter, the whole washed down with milk or weak tea.

You see, sour milk was one of the mainstays of our diet, for rich and poor alike. We call it *prostokvasha*. It is simply prepared. Just let ordinary fresh milk sour at room temperature, in a big bowl, until it reaches the consistency of junket. Then put it in the icehouse (or refrigerator) and let it become thoroughly chilled. Serve with bread crumbs or plain. In the cities we added sugar to it, but in the villages, where sugar was a luxury (thank God), it was eaten plain.

Lunch would be much the same. Big sandwiches, made out of the heavy, wholesome rye bread (white bread was a Sunday delicacy) and cottage cheese, or ordinary homemade cheese, or fish smoked in one's own smoking house, and hot tea or milk.

Supper consisted mainly of borsch, the celebrated Russian national soup, which is nothing more or less than vegetable soup made with meat stock and beetroots. With it was served whole-grained buckwheat porridge or millet.

Both porridges are prepared quickly and in the same manner. Take three cups of grains (for a family of four) and pour on it six cups of boiling water. Add salt to taste, and stick the bowl into the baking oven at 400 degrees.

Half an hour later, you will be rewarded with a glorious dish. Soft, downy porridge, each grain standing out alone, will fill your plate. Put on it nice big chunks of butter, or pour milk on it. Your teeth will grow white and strong. Besides, you will know you had a real-stick-to-your-ribs meal. We call these porridges *kasha*.

Borsch and kasha were the mainstay of Russia, plus the rye bread, the gallons of fresh milk, the fresh butter, and the tea with berry jam, made the previous summer — or a variation of this, with the kasha serving as a bed for a nice chunk of boiled beef that came out of the borsch! Wholesome, simple meals these are, with oceans of vitamins in the soup, from the slow-boiling vegetables and the meat stock. And the bread, indeed, has the staff of life in it, undevitalized and nourishing.

Vegetables were eaten in quantities, especially boiled beets, carrots, and cabbages. The latter was often salted for the winter and eaten as sauerkraut, another Russian favorite dish full of vitamins.

For dessert we had nuts and raisins. There was very little candy or sugar. Cake, as served here, was unknown. But we had many coffee cakes, made with yeast, out of whole-grained flour. Pies were a mystery too, but *pirogies* were a Sunday treat. These, as I have mentioned, were made out of yeast dough and were filled with sweetened cottage cheese or with cabbage cooked in butter until nicely browned or with mushrooms freshly gathered in the woods or even with minced meat — hamburger style, with onions!

All these would make my mouth water. I wonder if they would appeal to the sophisticated and refined palates of my friends.

Be that as it may, the fact remains that because of this diet the teeth of the people needed little or no attention. My aunt, at sixty, boasted she had all her own teeth. But no one was surprised, for there were millions of others in her age group who could also exhibit every tooth that nature had endowed them with.

Strangers would recognize easily all the usual farmer's buildings but one. They would quickly spot the barn, the pigsty, the chicken coops. But a little house standing rather close to the main *isba* would baffle them. Yet it was an essential for every Russian household.

It was called a *bania*, which means "bathhouse." And that's what it was. In it the visitor could find a little hallway, the walls of which were covered with wooden pegs to hang his clothing on. The next room had a structure made of stones. In the middle of this was cemented an immense caldron. Under that there was a large opening in which to build a fire. A sort of stone stove, with a big stone chimney.

Every Saturday morning the young people of the house would be seen lugging big chunks of wood into the bania, and many pails of water.

Saturday night, after work, was bath night in all Russian villages. Members of each family would take turns in the bathhouse. Throwing cold water on the overheated stone stove, they would get steam galore into the big room. Then, climbing on the wide benches, arranged like steps, they would literally steam themselves clean, either by simply lying still or by pounding themselves with birch switches to which fragrant green leaves still clung. The switches merely hastened the process of cleaning. You got just as clean without them, but it took longer.

One's whole body tingled with the clean sensation of its opened pores.

Then began the business of scrubbing and washing hair and body. Again and again hot, clean water was mixed with cold. And homemade soap — none ever smelled cleaner to me — was used in abundance. The whole performance was finished, in the winter, with a quick roll in the snow outside or with the dashing of a couple of buckets of ice-cold water over oneself.

Fresh and clean, clad in spotless, newly laundered clothing, the family would assemble for the special Saturday supper, consisting usually of tea, drunk by the gallon, bread, butter, and cheese or jam.

Sunday saw the whole village at church. Home afterward for the Sunday dinner and a nice rest for the older folks, followed later by a get-together on the village green. There the young people would start a square dance at a moment's notice or play Lapta. This somewhat resembles American baseball but is played with a polished oblong piece of wood instead of a ball. This is sent flying with a bat and the batter runs to the bases — the bases being much like the ones over here.

Laughter and jokes, singing and dancing, and playing various games — such was a Sunday afternoon and evening in a Russian village.

Winter changed the tempo and brought folks more indoors. Women oiled their spinning wheels and fixed their looms. Grannies started their knitting. With their chores done, the men made furniture, toys, or ornamental wooden boxes, or worked in their little copper and brass workshops.

Parties were held in the homes. The girls brought their embroideries, the boys their knives. Much storytelling took place while both worked. Much laughter was heard too. And some dancing would invariably follow.

Outside recreation was nonexistent, villages seldom being near railroads. The people, young and old, had to depend on themselves and their ingenuity to provide such recreation or amusement as was needed. And they did it, too — beautifully.

As in Ireland, the art of storytelling was highly valued. The true storyteller was a respected and loved member of any community. Some of them were country famous; for, fancy free and foot loose, they would often wander across the immense land, telling stories that were old, or inventing new ones, in palace and isba. They were usually welcomed in both.

Singing was another natural art in Russia. It is said there that a Russian is born to the tune of a song, sings his life through, and with a song is laid to rest. And that is true. Singing comes naturally to people who live close to nature. Russian songs with their undertones, now of deep sadness, now of riotous mirth, are well known abroad. To them, as to the folk tales, both composers and musicians in Russia have turned again and again for inspiration.

Dancing, alone or in groups, to steps handed down by one's forefathers, or to new steps invented as one went along, was as natural to most Russians as breathing. As tiny children they began it, and only the coffin stopped them.

Many a time I have seen a tiny shepherd, while watching his flock and playing a homemade reed flute, execute the most intricate and graceful steps on the green of hillside or plain.

Orchards and vegetable gardens formed a background of every village home. Bees were cultivated lovingly and knowingly. For honey was another staple of every man's diet. It was eaten "as is," and it was also constantly used in cooking. I think I could gather a small book of honey recipes, if I were put to it.

Yes, the village with its age-old pattern of life firmly established, with its artistic, cultural, and creative life flowing freely, and its just distribution of land, was the heart and the strength of Russia. And all its life truly centered around home and church.

It was a good life. Backward in one sense, perhaps — for its tools were simple, its hours long, and its work hard. Yet it was wholesome, and it made the nation strong with its deeply rooted Christian ideals and its almost indestructible family life.

No wonder that in my memories I constantly go back to the peaceful normal life of a Russian village.

There my weary heart can rest from the unstable, tragic conditions of family life and of society in our dark days.

Chapter Fifteen

CO-OPERATIVES

Co-operation in many forms was well known to Russia from old, old days. One of the seemingly strange forms of democratic government, which existed all through the years of the absolute monarchy, was the *Zemstvo*.

Zemstvo could be called the corporate voice of Russian villages. Officially they were under the Departments of Agriculture and Forestry.

There was, of course, in each village, a Council of Villagers, which dealt with the daily affairs of the village. A representative of each village was sent to the local organization of the Zemstvo, and together these spoke for a certain region. The regional Zemstvo Council had a national council to which a member was elected from each regional office. Thus the voice of the peasants was always heard through these councils, even by the Czar and his government.

Actually, however, though democratic in setup, once they reached the highest authority the word of the then reigning monarch, through his ministers, was final. But, even so, much attention was paid in high places to that voice that represented, indeed, the greatest part of the Russian population.

It was under the aegis of the Zemstvo that health education and health measures were promoted. Through them, again, agricultural education and aid were given. Merchandising of farm products was helped, and financial problems tackled. It was a powerful group, even in a monarchical setup.

It was through the Zemstvos that the co-operative movements were begun, through them and the workman's guilds, known as *artels*. Dairy, lumber, and grain co-ops were common throughout the land, and helped the producer to market his produce at equitable prices.

Early in the organization appeared the Consumer Co-ops, dotting the land both in small villages and large towns. I remember that my parents belonged to the Army-Navy Co-op Department Store in St. Petersburg. This would have rivaled any average department store on this side of the Atlantic.

Not only did the Navy and Army personnel organize their own co-ops but various other homogeneous groups also worked to spread this just, democratic way of trading.

By 1915 a whole network of co-operatives, both producers' and consumers', literally covered Russia; and the education this movement brings with it was reaching out into the most distant hamlets. Then, of course, credit unions slowly began to do their part in redistributing wealth. Being a neighbor of Sweden, Norway, and Denmark, where the Co-operative Movement was growing by leaps and bounds, Russia did not have far to go to learn better ways of co-operative life.

The Monarchist Government, strangely enough, protected the Co-op Movement, and afforded it many facilities. The Communists, though, from all recent information, abolished the movement and destroyed all that it had built up. One can easily understand that in a country where the government itself is producer, wholesaler, and jobber, there would be no room for co-operative movements.

I am sorry that, in my youth, I took this movement utterly for granted and never troubled to study its beginnings, so that today I am unable to give any real report on its wonderful work in Russia. But I feel sure that any reader interested enough can easily find out all these details, especially one who has access to the well-stocked libraries in our big cities.

All I wanted to do in this short chapter was to bear witness to the fact that this movement did exist; that it brought much help to all the people of Russia; and that it had the approbation and protection of a government, usually considered backward, barbaric, and opposed to all advances of science and education.

Chapter Sixteen

EDUCATION

There is one misconception that makes me rather angry when talking to the average non-European, and that is his idea of education in Russia.

The belief seems not only prevalent, but deep rooted, that the Russian masses at least, were illiterate; and that the Czarist government wanted them kept that way, for its very existence demanded that the masses be held as long as possible in the chains of ignorance.

This firmly rooted misconception holds that if there be anything good to say about the Communist regime, it is this — that, at least, it brought literacy to Russia.

I should not get excited. Such misconceptions grow out of ignorance. And until the end of World War II, and the beginning of Cold War I, nobody in this hemisphere was studying Russia. So how could anyone know the truth?

The truth was so different from the "general ideas."

Until the invasion of the Tartars, Russia held her own easily with the Western nations. Trade and peaceful embassies on both sides brought the two parts of the then existing world together.

However, while the West forged ahead, from late medieval times into the Renaissance, Russia was retarded because she was forced to act as a bulwark, a protecting wall, against the Mongolian invader who sought to conquer all of Europe.

Her fighting, her fending-off of the barbarian hordes, resulted in her being segregated from the West.

That was not the only sacrifice her fighting cost her.

No educational or intellectual pursuits of any kind could be developed or followed by a nation that spent all its days, months, years, and even centuries at war. Nor could any progress be made under the ruthless heels of conquerors whose nomadic ways had nothing of culture to give.

Between trying to fight off the Tartars and trying to find enough to eat, the Russians "wasted" *four hundred* years. True, in the time of Ivan the Terrible — and of Elizabeth of England — the hold of the Mongolian overlords was finally weakened, and Siberia was taken over and opened to Russian emigrants. But it was not until the advent of Peter the Great, who died in 1725, that Russia really could take a deep breath and wonder about the life to come.

She not only had finished with the Mongolians, but

Education

she also had repulsed her other enemies, the Swedes. She had annexed a great part of the Baltic territory and had thus reached her long-sought goal, the sea!

Now she could call the sea her own. On it, she could again send her products westward, without having to cross any enemy territory. On it, and by it, and because it was her own, she could take up her long-interrupted concourse with her Western neighbors. Outlets to the sea, incidentally, explain much of Russia's history, many of her wars, and much of her baffling foreign policies.

Only in the reign of Peter the Great could Russia start on something resembling peaceful pursuits, which included education. Czar Nicholas II was only some three hundred years removed from Peter.

Three hundred years is a short time in the life of a nation. Yet, around 1916, the world was already cognizant of the cultural stature of Russia. Tolstoy, Dostoevski, Pushkin, Lermontov, Turgenev, Gogol, and other writers of genius were being translated and read the world over. The Russian Ballet was taking Paris, London, and other European capitals by storm. Wherever good music was appreciated, Russian composers were leading the way. And Russian painters and other artists were making their contribution to the world's galleries, and were acclaimed in many lands. Repin, and Roerich, to name but two of them, had world-wide reputations.

Thus in less than three hundred years, Russia not only had caught up with many signs of Western culture but, in many of its aspects, led the way.

Meanwhile, the masses were receiving much attention along educational lines. Early in the twentieth century education had become compulsory. True, this law was not strictly enforced. It could not be. For before a nation can dot its acres with schoolhouses, it has to establish lines of communication and attend to its railroads and its arteries. This Russia was doing fast; but not fast enough, perhaps, for its size.

Nevertheless, long before Communism was heard of, seven million more children went to primary school every year than the year before. Moreover, literacy came to the Russian young men through conscription, to which each of them was subjected for three years. The Army and Navy taught every man the three "R's," together with the usual army routine. At the end of their term, millions of youths returned to their villages, much better educated than when they left it. And there were many opportunities open to them to continue the education thus forcibly begun.

The usual run of education was quite different from the English pattern. It was molded more on French and German ideas. Thus, there were two types of high schools. One was given over to the preparation of mathematicians, engineers, architects, and the like. There, mathematics and science predominated. This was called the "Realnaya School." The other was named the "Gymnasium School." In it the study of Latin, Greek, Hebrew, and modern languages predominated. Both demanded from their pupils the marks of educated men — a good wide knowledge of philosophy, history, literature, and religion.

The average curriculum of a Russian high school encompassed botany, zoology, chemistry, physics, and anatomy. In mathematics, the course led from simple arithmetic to algebra, geometry, trigonometry, and calculus. Literature was studied thoroughly; Russian extensively; French, English, and German, first in translations, then in the originals. History led the student from mythology, through ancient and medieval days, to modern times and gave him an extensive course in the story of his own country.

Religion held a prominent place in every curriculum. Catechism and the history of the Church were given in every school. Cosmology, philosophy, and theology were sketchily begun in high school, to be continued in university courses. Languages were taught by the Berlitz system and a combination now used by the American Army. They were taught by native teachers, graduates of universities in their own countries, fully qualified to teach and preferably without any knowledge of Russian. The textbooks were published in the language to be studied and were without any Russian translations.

Preliminary or grade school students started at the age of six. After four years, one went to the Realnaya or to the Gymnasium, and stayed there for eight years. Upon graduation one was eligible to the entrance examinations of a university, where much attention was paid to dictation and to religious knowledge.

One would fail in the first if one made more than four mistakes in punctuation. It was argued that the hallmark of a truly educated man is his ability to read and write his native tongue correctly; and also to understand the mother of all sciences, theology.

In the matter of denominations, the question was solved quite simply. Religious teachers of all faiths came together for the periods allotted for that subject into any given school. The students were divided according to their denomination, and classrooms were allotted for each. Thus, Jew, Catholic, Orthodox, and Protestant teachers gave their adherents such knowledge as was required.

There were, admittedly, certain divisions along class

lines. For instance, certain military schools and certain girls' schools were reserved strictly to the nobility. In one, admission was even made only to the sons and grandsons of generals and high-ranking noblemen. But by and large, education was democratic on the university level, and also in the high schools. In my "rather select" school, the daughter of a janitor once walked away with all the prizes.

Tuition was low. Scholarships were many. Medical schools were opened to women earlier than in some parts of the West.

One of my aunts was a well-known eye specialist.

Law did not bar women either. Race, color, or creed made little difference. With, alas! one exception. The Jew.

The treatment of the Jews is indeed a sad page in Russian history. Relegated, in fact segregated, into certain portions of the vast Russian land, these wonderful people could not travel freely about. They had to have special permits to go from one place to another, and especially to come and live in the capitals — Petrograd and Moscow. Universities accepted only 10 per cent of Jews to a given year of enrollment. However, once graduated, the Jewish student had the freedom of travel and residence.

Most of the educated and liberal Russians were deeply ashamed of this state of affairs. I remember my father's constantly bemoaning it, and doing all in his limited power to fight it. He taught his children love and respect not only for Jews, but for all people, reminding us constantly of the Incarnation and Redemption of our Lord Jesus Christ, which made all men brothers of one another.

Universities in Russia were utterly different from the

colleges and universities here. They boasted of no campus life. One just enrolled for such or such a course. And unless research or laboratory work were attached to the course, one was not even compelled to attend the lectures. There was no roll call. One received the mimeographed, or printed, lectures of his professor, and appeared in due time for the examinations posted.

Of course, it was different for chemists, engineers, architects, and the like, who had to put in so many hours of lab work or drawing. These were subjected to roll calls, having to have so many hours of the above.

Where did one live? What did one do in free hours? Was one married or single? These things did not concern the university faculties or governments. Teaching alone was their job. And the men and women attending courses were considered adults, and mature enough to look out for, and after, themselves.

The school day began at nine o'clock in the morning and went on usually to four o'clock, with five-minute recesses between hours and forty-five minutes for lunch — which was eaten at the school. About two hours of homework rounded out the student's day. That for primary classes.

The high schools followed the same pattern, and music was added to the curriculum, plus a heavy schedule of summer reading. When the student reached the university, he felt at home in research work. He had acquired habits of studiousness.

Lacking social life, as understood by the English-speaking college and university student, the Russians made up for it by forming debating societies, dramatic societies, reading societies, and political societies.

Taken by and large, the Russian university student was

quite mature, politically and socially. He was usually, too, an omnivorous reader in many extracurricular subjects. He was the catalyst of Russia. Often rebellious, keen on righting all wrongs, especially those of social justice, he was a crusader for many reforms. Because of his numbers, his voice, though young, was powerful. To him can be attributed the spearheading of many liberal movements, especially that of bringing a more democratic form of government to the land.

To finish the comparison on the academic level. A high school student graduating from one of the Russian schools would receive a B.A. or a B.S. in Canada or America. A Russian B.A. or B.S. would equal an M.A. or M.S. here. Correspondingly, an M.A. or M.S. would be equal to a Ph.D. in his field. This of course does not take in the difference of native tongues.

Given another decade or two, without wars or revolutions, Russia would have, in the normal course of events, caught up with her own vastness, and indeed brought universal compulsory education to her people. Thus the "achievements" along educational lines of the Communist regime — though undeniable — were possible only because of the preliminary work accomplished before they came to power.

One more question must be answered before this chapter is completed. What of religious education by nuns and monks or priests, as we know it in the West?

Alas, the answer to this must be, by and large, a negative one. The official Russian religion was that of the Russian Orthodox Church. As we all know, this Church separated itself from Rome in the tenth century, under the influence of a rebellious patriarch named Photius. It denies only two of the tenets common to both Churches, the infallibility of the pope and a complicated theological point concerning the Holy Ghost, known as "the Filioque question."

For details on both, I refer you to Mr. Attwater's concise and precise works on the Eastern Churches.

The Orthodox Church has the validity of both apostolic succession and the Sacraments. In time of gravest emergencies, such as danger of death, Catholics are allowed to go to confession to Orthodox priests and receive Viaticum from them. People married in the Orthodox Church are considered validly married by the Catholic Church; ordinations are also considered valid.

But its separation . . . its schism . . . has left, as was to be expected, an inner weakness in its works of grace. Missionaries are almost unknown in the Orthodox Church; and the religious education of the young never got under way except in the early ages of the Church's history, when, as in the whole world over, its monks and nuns held the keys to all available learning. For it was they, in the East as well as in the West, who painted the prayer books and the missals, and who taught the arts of reading and writing.

Art, religious art, was also in their hands. But, as time went on, monasteries and convents became all similar. The closest approach to their way of life in the West would be the early Benedictine Rule, somewhat exemplified by the Trappists now.

The rule was not so severe as to food and silence. It consisted of a combination of prayer, mostly liturgical, including the Divine Office, contemplation, and manual labor. The work was in the fields, in the barns and sheds, in the art shops, in the music rooms, and in the manuscript-illuminating cells.

The nuns lived somewhat after the fashion of the monks with the difference that their art work lay not so much in the ways of producing books as in turning out beautiful handicraft products, altar cloths, and ecclesiastical vestments.

Novitiates were always scattered affairs — young postulants and novices clustering in small groups around some "teacher" renowned for learning and for holiness.

The whole was something like life in the early Carthusian monasteries of the West!

In my Russian yesterdays the same pattern prevailed. Here and there one could find religious schools taking care of orphans or teaching young boys the art of farming and the three R's — with emphasis on religion — all with some expectation that the students would join the orders that taught them.

Roman Catholic or definitely Protestant schools were nonexistent in Russia. In Finland, of course, there were Protestant schools. And in Poland there were many Catholic schools. Russia ruled both Poland and Finland, but allowed each country to teach its own in its own religious way.

Perhaps the whole destiny of the world would have been altered had Orthodox monasticism developed along the vigorous educational lines of youth that the Roman Catholic Church followed in the West.

But then, the price of schism is weakness — and religious orders in Russia paid the price.

Chapter Seventeen

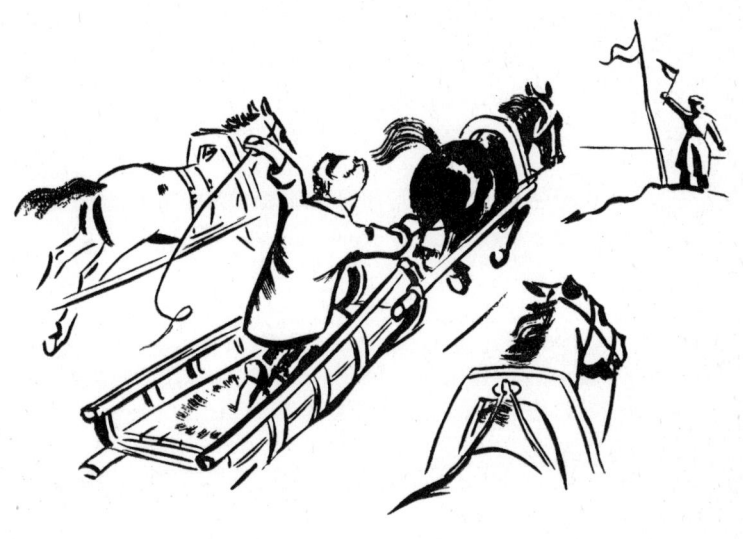

SPORTS

The Russians were, strangely enough, a rather individualistic people, and one that, owing to its long monarchical form of government, was not used to teamwork as it is known in more democratic countries.

Perhaps that had some effect on the development of sports. But sports never got commercialized. Probably the gate receipts would not justify it. Such sports as were played, remained, for the most part, on an amateur standing.

Among them, in urban centers, were tennis, soccer, and football. Golf had started with royalty. The Czar installed an eighteen-hole golf course on one of his summer estates. But the game never reached the peasants.

Gymnastics were held on a large scale, *à la* Czechoslovakia. The Sokols were popular with high school children, and there were public displays several times a year.

Tennis produced some good players who entered and often won in international tournaments. I myself played in a tournament against England. We lost, rather ingloriously.

Fishing and hunting were the Russians' real sports. The vast land, with its infinite variety of climates and geographical changes, lends itself ideally to them. There was deep-sea fishing in the Baltic, the Black, and the Caspian seas, and fresh-water fishing in the innumerable lakes and rivers. Russia was a fisherman's dream of paradise. And a hunter's.

I remember in my childhood Father and his friends hunting grizzlies and wild boar with knives and special spears. They felt it was sporting to hunt these animals with only such weapons. They would have thought it a sign of weakness or barbarism to carry rifles on these hunts.

Besides bears, wolves, and boars, the hunter could find plenty of moose, deer, partridges, wild ducks, and other game. The supply seemed inexhaustible, though everyone in Russia was a hunter.

On the large estates, hunts were often organized somewhat in the English hunting traditions, but with less show and style.

Turgenev rendered the Russian understanding and love of sport most beautifully and fully in his celebrated *Diary of a Sportsman,* which I highly recommend to all those interested in fishing and hunting.

Boxing was a favorite and a national sport. It was indulged in by all male Russians, until Queen Elizabeth, daughter of Peter the Great, forbade it as being too barbaric. And so it may have been, for it was conducted without rules and without gloves.

But not even the edict of a queen could stop the Russians from "boxing-in-the-raw." It was still in vogue in many villages in my yesterdays, though slowly the English type of boxing was becoming popular.

Wrestling was a sport that did "draw a gate"; and the only one I remember being commercialized.

Skating and skiing were natural for Russians. And skating tournaments, for amateurs, always, were very popular. Everyone skated. Skiing "caught on" slowly, for to most Russians it, like snowshoeing and rowing, was less a sport than a mere method of locomotion. It took a little time to get used to the idea that these three usual and necessary means of covering distance could be indulged in for fun or in competition. Our neighbors — the Finns, Norwegians, and Swedes — brought the idea to us. And Russians began to take to skis, snowshoes, and rowing as pure sport; and they began to participate in international matches, especially in skiing and rowing.

Horse lovers and traders from way back, the Russians were always at home on a horse; from time immemorial the Russian cavalry was known as one of the best in the world. Both military and private horse shows, and riding and hunting exhibits were loved and well attended by the Russians — and made the subject of wagers. Russians often competed in international horse shows and could exhibit, over a period of centuries, many a trophy gallantly won.

Horse racing was developed to a high degree. It was indeed the sport of kings. The land was literally dotted with race courses that would draw millions of spectators at certain seasons. My father raised trotters. He was at home in any sport connected with horses, even polo, which was quite popular with a certain class of people.

Hiking and bicycling as known in Europe was not popular in Russia. We were a nation of walkers — naturally. And bicycles? Well, bicycle races were occasionally held. But the Russian country roads were not ideal for bicycles. We'd rather walk than pedal over those roads.

We "hiked" thousands of miles, but it was mostly on pilgrimages. It was seldom we hiked for fun or just to get somewhere from somewhere else.

Our village youth played Lapta, the game which as I have already mentioned, was reminiscent of baseball. And they danced. If dancing be a sport, then it most assuredly was the favorite sport of Russia. The stately national dance and the fast square ones were everybody's favorites — from the village green to the palace. Ballroom dancing was seen only in the cities.

Chapter Eighteen

RECREATION

It's a strange thing about recreation. It seems to be of two kinds: one created by the folks themselves, and the other made for them to watch, a nonparticipation affair that tires more than it rests.

Frankly, in my Russian yesterdays I was used to the first type only. Much of every Russian's time was spent on the land, far away from any commercial nonparticipatory recreation. One simply had to fall back on one's own resources. That was fun indeed.

Oh, we did have the theater, the ballet, the opera, and the concerts. These attracted almost everyone — rich, poor, and in-between. For the theater, in all the above-mentioned phases of its art, was government-supported. All the artists were on the pay roll of the government. The government also made up any deficit that might occur at the end of any fiscal year.

Moreover, every artist had in his contract a clause that provided for extra performances outside the big theaters. He bound himself to play, sing, or dance in the Narodni halls, the people's theaters. In these theaters the populace could see any star and many outstanding plays, operas, or ballets for the equivalent of five cents.

Also there were summer tours through the country that brought outstanding talent into the smallest cities.

Artists were recruited from all stratas of society, and the government's scouts traveled the year around in search of young people with budding talent. This was before the Hollywood talent scout was ever heard of.

Once a young man or woman was selected by any of these scouts, he or she was offered a full education, even into the university, by the government, free of charge. Then at the end of this, there was the chance of obtaining a permanent contract, with a salary that would enable one to devote all his time to the perfecting of his work.

Of course, this education had an accent on whatever branch the youngsters were directed to by their natural ability. Thus if it were the ballet, one would have to know all about dancing, and to dance. If it were drama, the education would embrace the fundamentals of that art. If it were singing, music would play the major role in the curriculum.

Perhaps this could be done under a monarchical or Communist regime. For this is the pattern followed even today in Russia. I remember when the Moscow Art

Theater was preparing to produce Gorki's *Dno* (*The Depths*). The cast was given six months to go into the depths, the slums of Moscow, to learn at firsthand how the denizens dressed, spoke, and acted — a procedure, I think, that would be impossible of achievement under the profit and loss system which prevails in private enterprise. But the results, as the whole world knows, are magnificent. Among them are the unique Russian Ballet, the Moscow Art Theater, and the Russian Opera with its outstanding singers of whom Chaliapin is best known abroad.

The theater was an old, old love of the Russians. And there was many a little group of amateur players in every part of the land. In my yesterday, movies were just coming in. But this new medium of entertainment was known only to the big cities and was not too well liked.

In the old day, the nobility, who lived almost the year around on their estates, had their own elaborate theaters and their actors. Each noble family vied with the others to produce better plays or stage more perfect ballets. This love of the drama, the opera, and the ballet, for all three forms were always linked together in the Russian heart, helped the development of writing talent. I fervently hope that the day will come when the history of the Russian Theater will be fully written for the world to read and enjoy.

Singing — choral, choir, and group — was another art that the Russians excelled in, and that formed, together with solo singing, one of the major forms of recreation that seemed to come naturally to the whole nation. Church choirs were a specialty one traveled many a mile to hear. No organ was ever heard in Orthodox churches. Often the entire congregation, familiar with the whole services, would participate with the choir.

Male choirs, such as the Cossacks, well known abroad, or the Red Army Choir that toured Europe, were an integral part of my Russian yesterdays. They were also an integral part of almost every village, and, most assuredly, of the Army.

Women formed their own choirs, but often groups of men and women sang together.

I can still see the pastel shades of our northern spring. A big bonfire. And the village choir singing by its clear flames song after song from the inexhaustible repertoire of our folk tunes.

The guitar and the balalaika were instruments of accompaniment in individual singing, so beloved by the Russians. The old-timers used a type of zither to accompany themselves in their storytelling evenings, which were not exactly storytelling, but half telling and half singing affairs.

Games, singing, dancing, and the drama formed the majority of our recreation. But how much creativeness went into each! There was room in them for every member of the family, from Grandma and Grandpa to the newest toddler. Poor and rich took part. Servants and masters played and had fun side by side.

The past and the present met the future in storytelling, song, and dance. Minds were refreshed by planning and performing; and one's heart, soul, and mind, one's whole body was indeed *re-created* — made fresh and ready for another day's work. Together with our sports, it made the background of Russian leisure. And it was good. I miss it, and still try to pass on its beauty and freshness to the young folks who come to me to learn to live a fuller Christian life.

Chapter Nineteen

CUSTOMS

Customs . . . where did they originate? Why did they integrate themselves into the lives of this nation or that? Why do they cling so tenaciously to one's heart and mind? Why do they form part of one's own substance, set one apart from all other people and nations, and put on one their seal of "belonging"?

Perhaps somewhere, someone has answered these questions, but I have not as yet come across the answers. All I know is that the ways and customs of my people cling to me wherever I go. Almost unconsciously I follow them, patterning my life according to their familiar designs.

Some of them, I know, stem from religious observances, Christian or pagan; others just do not seem to have any beginnings that I know of. But all have a hold on me that, I suppose, death alone will break. I am glad of it, for they make my life fuller and richer, and somehow bring home to me the brotherhood of men under the Fatherhood of God.

For into my new adopted country I bring the old folkways of my people, sharing them with my new brothers and sisters of Canada and the United States. They, in turn, teach me their customs and ways. We get to know each other better, in a more intimate way, love each other more, and understand each other more easily, all of which goes to bring us closer together. And that is good.

Take traveling, for instance. Would anyone in old Russia venture on a journey without a supply of holy water? Of course, I have spoken before this of the love and veneration my people have for the sacramentals of the Church, but it bears repeating. For it seems that Catholics today have forgotten the powerful help in these. It is a pity they are relegated today to convents and monasteries only. Perhaps the old Russians have something to teach us here. For most assuredly, in the old days, no one would undertake any journey without holy water. We had a strange real understanding — a special grace of God, indubitably — of the prince of evil and his dangerous ways. Both were close to us, and we guarded against them assiduously.

That is why the family sat all together before undertaking the journey and prayed. A Hail Mary to Our Lady of the Travelers — an invocation for help to St. Raphael, and to the Angel Guardian — one was not afraid then of anything, for surely this was good company to have on the journey. We made sure they shared the journey with us. Even when we were to go alone, we first sat and prayed.

Would anyone in old Russia live in an unblessed house or apartment? Not likely. For it would be empty, a desolate place, where sorrow, pain, and sickness would come to dwell. People living there would be without the strength of Faith, Hope, and Charity (not to mention the immense benefits and graces that come with a priestly blessing). How could they carry the cross joyfully?

Who, in any Russian village, in the length and breadth of the whole land, would dare to plow and harrow an unblessed field? Or seed it with unblessed grain? No one but an infidel.

And the feast days! So many of them are marked forever in my heart with ways and customs that made them both holy and gay. A joy forever!

St. John the Baptist's Day, for illustration, was celebrated with huge bonfires. They seemed to reach the very skies, and they always brought out daring young men who jumped through dancing flames. Strangely enough they all came out unscathed and untouched by those fiery and dangerous fingers! Probably each whispered a quick prayer to the fearless saint.

On the same day the girls would weave beautiful wreaths from the many field flowers that bloomed about that time of the year. Laden with them, they would go to the nearest river or lake and, taking careful aim, throw them into the water to the accompaniment of age-old verses whose origin was lost in the dimness of centuries gone by. These rhymes expressed their hopes and desires.

This rite performed, the girls would run along the banks, a colorful and beautiful crowd, dressed in their native costumes. Each would watch her own wreath breathlessly, for the wreath that kept afloat longest promised its owner marriage within the year. And where is the young heart that does not yearn for love and romance?

The great feast of the Most Holy Trinity was also called the Green Feast in my youth. Then the Church and many of the homes were decorated with freshly cut green boughs — the color of spring and hope, and of love, and of God which to us were synonymous. But it was also the day of the *birch*. The village youth would gather at eventide and, with special songs and much laughter, go in search of the nearest and prettiest birch tree. The girls then, with the help of the boys, would decorate it with multicolored ribbons and flowers. The task accomplished, they would dance around it, special dances, to special old songs that have been taught from generation to generation. The boys at certain intervals were allowed to take a ribbon off the tree and pair off with the girl it belonged to. Many a true romance started there and then. No wonder the birch is the national Russian tree.

Old and new were intimately and strangely interwoven in Russia. Many pagan customs survived and were "baptized" by the Church. But once in a while, the Church permitted her children to perform, *strictly in fun,* some "unbaptized ones."

Among such was the "witching week," the week between Christmas and the feast of the Circumcision. To me this is still the gayest time of the year, and many are the girls and boys to whom I have taught the ways of that witching time. It's all in fun, of course, but they seem to love it too.

Do you want to find out whom you are going to marry, maybe this year? Well, that is simple. Take a mirror, not too large a one, and two candlesticks with tapering candles in them. Then retire into a barn or a distant room or an attic. Set the mirror on some table, and put the candles close to it, leaving the rest of the room in utter darkness. Concentrate. Be still. Look into the mirror without taking your eyes for even a split second from it.

In due time . . . it may be a minute, it may be many hours . . . you will see your "intended" come to you . . . *in the mirror*. It takes perseverance and time . . . and courage. . . . Have you got these?

Want to know your future? In fun, of course. Get some wax . . . melt it. When it is all liquid, throw it into a basin of cold water. If nothing else, you will be rewarded with the sight of the most fantastic and beautiful patterns you ever saw. Now gently lift the whole piece out . . . don't break any of it. Slowly, carefully, hold it against a wall so that it throws a clear shadow. A candle held at a certain angle behind it may help.

Watch the shadows carefully. They will "tell" you your future for the coming year . . . if you have imagination, that is, and can read shadows. But who can't, when one is young?

Want more of same? Take an old tray. Crumple a piece of paper. A newspaper will do. Set a match to it. Hold the tray steadily. Be sure there is no draft anywhere near by. Let it burn out. You will have a brittle mass of ashes that hold together. Repeat with the candle for proper light . . . and watch the wall. . . . This will give you shadows too . . . to read . . . and to dream of . . . about your future. It is fun too.

Are you the very curious type? Curious and bold? One who wants to know *all*? Including the name of your future husband . . . or wife? All right. Get ready. Dress warmly, and go out into the cold winter night, into the street, or the nearest country road. Wait for the next passer-by of the opposite sex. Stop him or her. Ask the name . . . that is the name you are looking for.

Anchorites. In the West they are but a name to be found in very old religious books or in new ones speaking of the early ages of the Church. Perhaps Russia was the only country that still had them in my youth; and I would not be at all surprised to learn that they are still there, living in the virgin woods that are even yet so plentiful in that immense land.

Though they are not exactly a "custom" of my people, they are part of its national life. That is why I want to discuss them in this chapter. For these solitaries, who left their monasteries with the permission of their abbots or other superiors, for one year or many, to dwell in solitude in the wild places, were much beloved by my people. And they expressed this veneration and love in thousands of ways.

No matter how far such a *holy one* might go to hide himself and dwell in prayer, fasting, and penance, the rumor of his presence would travel to the nearest village. From there, by word of mouth, it would go through the whole land. And there would always be someone to bring him food and drink. . . . Then later the sick were brought to him. And the sorrowful would seek him out, for advice, blessing, and consolation.

I saw one myself once, just after his return to the monastery of his origin. He had come back at the bidding of his superior. He was thin to the point of emaciation. His face was literally transparent; and through it shone a guiltless soul, a radiance. He was as one set apart, glowing with humility, gentleness, and the love of God and man.

As I knelt at his feet for his blessing, I felt healed, renewed, and joyful in the Lord.

No wonder people loved and cherished the *lonely ones* so. No wonder, too, that their presence was considered, and indeed was, a blessing! Thus it seemed that no matter where one turned, in Russia, there was a blessing of God to be found. Houses, fields, cattle, bees, forests, waters, fruits, harvests, vehicles, machinery, children, women, men, food — all reflected the blessing of God, His Church, and His priests. Added to all this was the blessing of the presence of the silent anchorites, who kept alive, under obedience, the penitent ways of the early Church.

Speaking of blessings, I wonder if my Catholic friends realize the blessing of a vigil light? I have mentioned them several times through this book, because they still "bless" every place I ever live in.

There is something about their flickering soft light, burning steadily before a favorite statue or ikon, that makes any room or any house, be it ever so humble or ever so magnificent, truly "blessed." Perhaps this is because the light so constantly and so faithfully reminds one of God and the things of God. Or maybe it is because we left it there as a more constant prayer than we ourselves could give, who are so busy.

Be it as it may, the loved and constantly present vigil light that always burned in Russian homes, and still does in mine, brought — and still brings — God and our Lady closer, makes one feel secure and at peace.

Yes, it is good to have them around.

It is good, too, to have special foods for special feasts and special days. I have spoken much of them already, but I would like to go on talking about them. For they are accents that make a certain day stand out, separate and vivid, apart from other days. That is why, again, wherever I am, I cook them.

I often go to great lengths to get together the proper ingredients for these special dishes. Hard or easy, they eventually grace my humble board on the appointed day, to the delight of friends and strangers, especially when their significance, spiritual or historical, is made clear.

I was so glad to read that beautifully written book, *Cooking for Christ*, written by Mrs. Florence Berger and published by the National Catholic Rural Life Conference, for it made clear the connection of many national customs with the liturgy of the Church, and hence with God. For in God all things come together — if properly used — to render glory to Him who is the Author of them.

And what education, what fun and joy, these old ways and customs of my people were for the children and young ones! How easily they learned through them to love and serve God better!

Even if certain customs were not exactly connected with Christianity, they made history live for many of the young.

May our Blessed Lady, whose shrines form so beautiful a rosary around the land of my forefathers, bring Russia back to her Father's house, and give back to her people the right to enjoy the old, holy, and joyous ways of their ancestors that made every year a new adventure in living and being.   Amen.

As I knelt at his feet for his blessing, I felt healed, renewed, and joyful in the Lord.

No wonder people loved and cherished the *lonely ones* so. No wonder, too, that their presence was considered, and indeed was, a blessing! Thus it seemed that no matter where one turned, in Russia, there was a blessing of God to be found. Houses, fields, cattle, bees, forests, waters, fruits, harvests, vehicles, machinery, children, women, men, food — all reflected the blessing of God, His Church, and His priests. Added to all this was the blessing of the presence of the silent anchorites, who kept alive, under obedience, the penitent ways of the early Church.

Speaking of blessings, I wonder if my Catholic friends realize the blessing of a vigil light? I have mentioned them several times through this book, because they still "bless" every place I ever live in.

There is something about their flickering soft light, burning steadily before a favorite statue or ikon, that makes any room or any house, be it ever so humble or ever so magnificent, truly "blessed." Perhaps this is because the light so constantly and so faithfully reminds one of God and the things of God. Or maybe it is because we left it there as a more constant prayer than we ourselves could give, who are so busy.

Be it as it may, the loved and constantly present vigil light that always burned in Russian homes, and still does in mine, brought — and still brings — God and our Lady closer, makes one feel secure and at peace.

Yes, it is good to have them around.

It is good, too, to have special foods for special feasts and special days. I have spoken much of them already, but I would like to go on talking about them. For they are accents that make a certain day stand out, separate and vivid, apart from other days. That is why, again, wherever I am, I cook them.

I often go to great lengths to get together the proper ingredients for these special dishes. Hard or easy, they eventually grace my humble board on the appointed day, to the delight of friends and strangers, especially when their significance, spiritual or historical, is made clear.

I was so glad to read that beautifully written book, *Cooking for Christ*, written by Mrs. Florence Berger and published by the National Catholic Rural Life Conference, for it made clear the connection of many national customs with the liturgy of the Church, and hence with God. For in God all things come together — if properly used — to render glory to Him who is the Author of them.

And what education, what fun and joy, these old ways and customs of my people were for the children and young ones! How easily they learned through them to love and serve God better!

Even if certain customs were not exactly connected with Christianity, they made history live for many of the young.

May our Blessed Lady, whose shrines form so beautiful a rosary around the land of my forefathers, bring Russia back to her Father's house, and give back to her people the right to enjoy the old, holy, and joyous ways of their ancestors that made every year a new adventure in living and being.   Amen.